The use of definite and indefinite reference in
young children

TO MY MOTHER AND FATHER

X.

WITHDRAWN

The use of definite and indefinite reference in young children

An experimental study of semantic acquisition

MICHAEL P. MARATSOS

Associate Professor of Child Psychology, Institute of Child Development, University of Minnesota

CAMBRIDGE UNIVERSITY PRESS

CAMBRIDGE

LONDON · NEW YORK · MELBOURNE

401.9
M3llu
1976

Published by the Syndics of the Cambridge University Press
The Pitt Building, Trumpington Street, Cambridge CB2 1RP
Bentley House, 200 Euston Road, London NW1 2DB
32 East 57th Street, New York, NY 10022, USA
296 Beaconsfield Parade, Middle Park, Melbourne 3206, Australia

ISBN: 0 521 20924 2

First published 1976

Photoset by Interprint (Malta) Ltd
and printed in the United States of America
by Colonial Press Inc., Clinton, Massachusetts

CONTENTS

TABLES

PREFACE

The central theme of this book is semantic acquisition — more particularly, a detailed experimental study of young children's competence in a small but rich aspect of semantics. The experimental work that forms the basis for the study was performed in 1971. It was then generally believed (and perhaps still is) that compared to how quickly they acquired the systax of their native language, children's acquisition of word meanings is slow and unimpressive (Anglin, 1970; McNeill, 1970). I do not believe that it is; extensive vocabulary acquisition may go on for many years. But what the child acquires in the preschool years I think will be shown to be enormously complex and impressive itself. This monograph is meant to be a part of the evidence for that assertion.

At the time of this study, R. Brown had been engaged for some time in the analysis of data for the first volume of *A first language* (1973). In the second half of that work, he considered various aspects of three children's acquisitions of a number of 'small' morphemes and inflections in English, such as the prepositions *in* and *on*, the progressive verb ending *-ing*, present and past tense, and the English articles *a* and *the*. It soon became apparent that in acquiring the stable use of these morphemes, children made semantic formulations of remarkable complexity in the preschool years. Two of the morphemes that seemed particularly complex were the indefinite and definite articles *a* and *the*. This was surprising, for they seem often like scarcely more than syntactic fillers. Yet considering their semantics, as I did for some months, soon made it apparent that their use required the child to be quite clever and to deal with abstract matters. A brief account is given of their use in the first part of the monograph, as an introduction to the difference between saying *a cat* and *the cat*, which turns out not to be a simple matter at all.

The naturalistic data indicated that the young children Brown was studying clearly knew something about the use of articles. As I discuss later, however, the full abstract range of their use could not be judged from looking at their conversations at home. Too often the conversations of young children are about immediately present contexts, and the proper use of articles and their related terms goes far beyond that. The question became one of whether from their more limited experience the children had been able to abstract more far-ranging principles of their use. It seemed clear that the study required experimental study. What the home situation did not conveniently offer for inspection would be elicited outside the home.

Experimental studies, however, always present their own problems. Anyone who has worked with preschool children, particularly children who are just three years old, can appreciate the difficulty of working with them as subjects. Excitement, boredom, misunderstandings, or inattention are all possible reactions to an experimental situation which may easily result in young children performing poorly in experimental tasks, worse than the competence they show simultaneously in spontaneous speech. Thus, in these studies, attempts were made to ensure that the children were at ease (a home visit was made before the experimental procedure), attentive (a quiet experimental room was used for the procedure), and interested (procedures were selected which the children seemed to enjoy).

A more important criticism of the experimental technique is that the procedure may fail to elicit children's knowledge because the experimenter takes for granted a mobility in their competence that may indeed be assumed when working with adult subjects, but not in working with children. Indeed, much of the evidence for the claim that children's lexical acquisition was slow came at the time of these studies from cross-sectional experimentation that used complex tasks such as word clustering or following a sentence read under noise (Anglin, 1970; McNeill, 1970). When a young child fails in a given procedure and older children or adults show competence, the experimenter will naturally conclude that the younger children have no competence at all. This seems often clearly unwarranted. Certainly the study of the development of general competence through specific tests is legitimate and useful, but we must be constantly wary of what is actually being explored in experimental studies. It is surely a truism that any experimental procedure can be raised to such a level of difficulty that everyone (with the natural exception of a few psychologists, linguists, and philosophers) will fail to show the tested competence. But with the exception of riddle jokes, no one intends to do so. I suspect, however, that the use of unintentionally difficult procedures often occurs, as outlined in more detail in later discussions in the book.

In the present study, then, the problems were investigated with a multiplicity of methods, in the hope that more of the truth about children's knowledge would emerge. A related aspect lies in the long piloting of procedures. As many children were seen in the process of devising the experimental tasks as were seen in the final experimental phase. Not infrequently what seemed to me like a perfectly reasonable procedure would prove by comparison with others to misfire completely, to fail to engage the child's knowledge at all. Certainly no claim is made that the methods are exhaustive, even for the study of articles. But they are varied, and the result of a long winnowing.

A major resulting theme of the monograph is the variation that different procedures may induce in what can abstractly be described as a unitary competence; at the same time it often becomes possible to elicit from the variegated results of the procedures some understanding of why this should be so. The overall procedure might be analogized to a geologist drilling out soil samples over a fairly wide area to determine the history of one small section of the earth. Unfortunately, for it to be an honest analogy the poor geologist must be forced to use different equipment and different bits for every attempt (and probably not be allowed to know how far down his drill has penetrated). He will then have a rather motley collection of samples, not at all as easy to organize; but by comparing his samples not only to each other, but also to the equipment used to procure each of them, he can still probably say a lot about the general lay of the land.

The point of variation induced by different procedures has some general importance as well. Recent proposals for studying semantic acquisition (Clark, 1973; 1974) plausibly suggest that one may learn much about how a child acquires lexical items by studying his natural strategic responses in contexts in which the items can be used. (For example, one might study whether an infant will naturally prefer to place something in or on an object that offers opportunities for both placements, in order to predict the order in which he will later acquire the terms *in* and *on*.) But if we can show — and I believe it is partly shown in the studies reported here — that variations in experimental situations may induce systematic changes in the child's responses in non-obvious ways, it becomes more difficult to make simple extrapolations from a child's responses in particular situations to the wider range of those contexts in which he actually acquires language.

Simultaneously, through tapping different and widespread uses, the studies here give an indication of the depth and abstractness of much of what the child must acquire of semantics. The approach is a narrow, intensive one: concentrated study of a small area of semantics rather than a broad study of a multitude of related terms. Whether or not the child's semantic growth terminates later than his syntactic growth, and other questions relating to the broad growth of the lexicon, can naturally not be studied in this way. But the narrowness and intensive quality of the approach makes it possible to produce a more deeply etched picture of the child's knowledge. In particular, the complexity of what children must acquire in their early learning of lexical semantics often finds its clearest delineation by this means, and an appreciation of this complexity seems to me an important aspect of understanding the nature of the human mind and its early development.

May 1975   MICHAEL P. MARATSOS

ACKNOWLEDGEMENTS

Many people have helped in bringing this study, essentially based on my doctoral dissertation, to its final form. I would like to express thanks here to:

Professor Roger Brown, who must be placed foremost among them. Without his wise, interested, and patient counsel, this work would have been largely without any of its present virtues.

Professor Eric Wanner, who was always willing to discuss with me issues of the study, and helped sharpen my intuitions about what they were and how to approach them.

Mr Ronald Kaplan, who first introduced to me much of the theoretical linguistic work which is basic to the thesis, and who is largely responsible as well for the rationale and form of the experimental procedures employed in chapter 4.

Professors Marshall Haith and Donald Olivier, who gave me valuable advice in the planning and carrying out of the analyses.

Professor David McNeill, who through his discussions and writings first aroused my strong interest in the field of language development.

Professors George Lakoff and John Ross, who through their thoughtful teaching of linguistics sustained and extended this interest.

Many friends who listened patiently to my woes and enthusiasms while the study was being completed, and gave me the benefit of their adult linguistic intuitions as well. These included Mr Thomas Considine, Ms Pam English, Mr Howard Gardner, Ms Deborah Holmes, and Ms Juliet Vogel.

Ms Esther Sorocka, who helped in the scheduling and obtaining of subjects for the study.

Ms Kay Adams, who skillfully prepared the final draft of the manu-script.

Finally, large numbers of children and many of their parents, who played odd games and answered peculiar questions with good grace and cheer.

1
Theoretical background

The semantics of articles

'Draw something', a child says to his mother.
'All right, what do you want me to draw?'
'Draw a horse.'

'Draw something', a child says to his mother.
'All right, what do you want me to draw?'
'Draw the horse.'

Thus on the distinction between *a* and *the* hangs the existence of a horse. For the first child, no special horse need serve as model for the drawing. But the case is quite different with the child who requests 'Draw the horse.' Without knowing more, we can guess that there is a horse conspicuous in the environment to serve as a model, a particular horse that the child expects to see drawn.

The indefinite and definite articles, *a* and *the*, do not seem like an auspicious place to study the semantic knowledge of young children. They are not semantic or syntactic building blocks of a language, like nouns, verbs, or adjectives, or even markers for tense. Yet they draw on and demand of the speaker mastery of referential systems of surprising complexity. They demand of the child, should he be born into a community that employs them, the formulation of correspondingly sophisticated semantic systems.

Part of what the child must learn is the distinction between existence and non-existence, but this is not quite the distinction required. The relevant difference is *particularity*, or *specificity*. Generally, the use of a definite article signals the reference to a very particular member of the class. Reference to particular class members may be called *specific* reference (Brown, 1973; Maratsos, 1971). A class member referred to specifically has distinctive properties which distinguish it from all members of that class. When saying *the X*, a speaker has in mind not just any instance of *X*, but a particular *X*.

Indefinite articles seem to command the residual: they refer to no particular member of the class or set named. In some instances the reference may be to no member of the class at all, but only to the notion of one. *Draw a horse* provides such an instance, as do negative sentences like *I haven't got a car*. No member of the classes *horse* or *car* is meant at all. In other cases the speaker intends reference to an existent member of the class, but a member not marked out by any properties aside from its being a member of the class. We can imagine a mother asking her child 'I've got your dresses here. What do you want to wear?' Should her child reply 'Give me a short dress', presumably she has some short dresses. But the indefinite article signals that she has no particular member of the class *short dress* in mind; any instance will do. The case is similar when a child says 'I want *a cookie*', or 'Read me *a book*.' A reference to no particular member of the class, or to no member at all, may be called *non-specific* reference.

In formulating the proper use of articles, the child must at least formulate their use consistent with the abstract distinction between specific and non-specific reference to members of a class. But this description leaves out still another central aspect of the definite—indefinite semantic system. That aspect is the shared knowledge of the speaker and his listener of the conversational referents. Suppose a child comes into his house from the street, having been bitten by a strange dog. He walks in and tells his mother, crying, 'The dog bit me.' 'What dog?' she replies, looking around or outside. The child's use of the definite expression implies she will know what dog he means already, but she does not. This example of a failure of communication is hypothetical, but Brown (1973) cites real instances between children and their parents.

> Sarah: The cat's dead.
> Mother: What cat?
>
> Adam: Put it up, the man says.
> Mother: Who's the man?

A definite reference to *the X* on the part of the speaker requires not only that he intend a uniquely specified member of *X*, but also that the reference to *the X* be specific for his listener. *The X* should bring to the mind of both speaker and listener the same particular, unique member of *X* as referent for the expression. When this condition is not filled, the listener may be puzzled because he is unable to bring to mind a previously specified, unique member of *X* to correspond to the listener's definite reference.

Ensuring specificity for the listener

How can the child make certain that his listener understands a reference with the same specificity as he does? There are a number of ways. Some references are specific for all even without further specification because of their general uniqueness. Such references include *the sun* or *the moon* or *the ground*. In various social groups references will be specific for all because of shared knowledge of the members of the group. In a house with a dog for a pet, a reference to *the dog* will be easily comprehended, as will a reference to *the car* in a family with one car. Some references are specific because of the conspicuousness of their referent in the immediate environment. In a living room, *the couch* generally refers unambiguously. Or pushing a table, it is clear what is meant by *the table* in asking 'Where should we put *the table*?' Sometimes a speaker may be able to take precautions to ensure that his reference is understood. If he has a particular table in mind out of a number in the room, he may point to the table or act on it some other way to make it conspicuous. Or he may elaborate the class description so that only one member is present, by saying something like 'Let's put this on *the table over by the piano*.' Where *table* may not make specific reference, *the table over by the piano* might. Specificity of reference does not inhere in the object referred to, but in the relation between the object and the class membership description given by the linguistic expression. Of course the same speaker can participate in varying contexts, and the meaning of his references changes accordingly. In the United States generally, reference to *the president* without further description reliably means the current chief executive officer of the country. To a group of academicians discoursing on university affairs, a reference to *the president* could easily mean the university executive.

Conversationally introduced specificity

The problem often arises, however, that a reference specific for the speaker cannot be made specific for his conversant by any of the above means, not by socially shared knowledge or by induced physical conspicuousness. The problem becomes more pointed in speaking of a referent neither already known to the listener nor physically present.

The speaker must then use purely conversational means to lend specificity to the reference for his listener.

What the speaker must do in such a case is introduce the referent with what can be called a *specific indefinite* expression. Though the intended reference is specific for himself, the speaker nevertheless defers to his listener's lack of knowledge of the particular referent intended by initial indefinite reference. Consider again the instance of the boy described above who had been bitten by a strange dog on the street. It was inappropriate for him to tell his mother immediately 'The dog bit me.' What would be appropriate is an indefinite introduction for the dog: '*A dog* bit me', or 'There was *a dog*, and *The dog* bit me.' The use of the indefinite reference indicates to his mother that he is referring to a member of the class of dogs not already known to her. When the speaker's reference is specific for himself but not for his listener, such an introductory indefinite reference becomes appropriate.

Once a referent in a discourse has become established as a unique member of its class for both speaker and listener in the discourse, future references to it should be definite ones, such as *the dog*. Such referents are referred to by Karttunen (1968a,b) as *discourse referents*: a referent that is to be referred to specifically in the discourse for both speaker and listener.

Specificity by entailment
It may seem as though the kind of specificity involved in a conversation about absent referents differs sharply from the perceptual specificity provided in a conversation about physically present referents, especially given the different means of establishing discourse referents in each. But the two kinds of situations are actually closely linked. The case of *entailment*, discussed by Karttunen (1968b), provides a clear conceptual bridge between the two types of context. The workings of entailment follow from the fact that simply mentioning some referents or situations necessarily entails the existence of other, immediately specified referents, which can themselves become discourse referents. Karttunen exemplifies the workings of entailment in a hypothetical discourse:

> I was driving on the freeway the other day when suddenly *the engine* began to make a funny noise. I stopped *the car* and when I opened *the hood*, I saw that *the radiator* was boiling (Karttunen, 1968b, p. 10).

It was not necessary for the speaker to introduce the car, hood, and radiator as discourse referents by means of introductory specific indefinite expressions, e.g. 'I was driving *a car*. It has *a hood* and *a radiator*.' All of the italicized definite expressions in the passage are properly definite without such introduction because driving on a freeway entails the existence of a particular car that was driven. In turn the existence of the car entails a hood, radiator, and engine belonging to the car. Speakers use words when conversing about absent referents to construct situations. Discourse referents can be created or prepared in conversations without the use of overt verbal introduction and treated referentially much like those in physically present contexts. The rules of definite and indefinite reference apply similarly through different kinds of discourse, with the addition that specific indefinite expressions may be necessary to introduce a referent to the listener when no other means suffices.

Summary of the semantics

A child learning the use of definite and indefinite articles, then, must formulate a semantic system both abstract and sensitive to discourse variables such as his listener's likely knowledge of particular referents. The categories of reference we have been discussing are summarized in table 1.1, which has been adapted from Brown (1973) with somewhat different examples. The upper left-hand quadrant corresponds to instances in which the speaker has in mind a particular member of the class and is confident that his listener will be able to understand the expression he uses as referring to just the same unique member or the class. A reference such as *the dog* is appropriate only when specific in this way for both speaker and listener. The lower left-hand quadrant

Table 1.1. *The relation between definite and non-definite forms and specific and non-specific reference in speaker and listener*

	Speaker specific	Speaker non-specific
Listener specific	Definite: *the* Where should we put *the table*? *The engine* began to make a funny noise.	Null (?)
Listener non-specific	*A dog* bit me. There's *a table* over here.	Draw *a horse*. I haven't got *a car*.

corresponds to the case in which the reference is specific for the speaker but not for his listener. In this divergence of viewpoints, the speaker must defer to his listener's lack of knowledge and refer with an indefinite expression. The lower right-hand quadrant exemplifies the case in which reference is specific for neither speaker or listener: any member of the class may be intended, as in 'Give me *a short dress*', or the referent may be non-existent, as in 'I haven't got *a car*.'

(The table makes clear a fourth logical possibility aside from the three major categories of reference we have discussed, a case in which reference is thought by the speaker to be specific for his listener, but not for himself. The speaker imagines that the listener may understand a reference specifically when he, the speaker, does not. For example, the speaker might suspect someone of harboring a spy in the basement of his house but not be certain. The case is a problemetical one, and in any case, the category is not a central one for our concerns.)

Naming

The discussion of the preceding pages is useful for pointing out central characteristics of the definite—indefinite referential system that children must learn. It is certain, however, that no short discussion of a complex semantic can ever be complete. Few semantic systems display an inclination to be neatly summarized by the enumeration of a few principles. Appendix xi contains a discussion of several important but problematical instances where the freedom of the speaker and listener to strain or violate these conventions is apparent and where the conventions apply only with some lack of grace. One of the problematical instances, however, is too basic not to be discussed here, and that is the case of *naming* or *nomination*, one of the essential operations of reference. Brown (1973) states the problem clearly:

> When pointing and naming something new, a thing both parents
> and children often do, one says *That's a train* or *That's a bear* and
> then goes on to use the definite forms: *it* or *the train* or *the bear*.
> Why does the introductory sentence use a non-definite form?
> Nominatives of this sort are used in situations in which both
> speaker and listener are attending to the same specific referent,
> and, in addition, the speaker is likely to be pointing at it. I.e., it
> seems as though reference should be in the definite (p. 347).

Brown believes that such instances fall into the category of references specific for the speaker but not the listener. The speaker pointing out the name knows that it applies to the conspicuous train or bear, but the listener presumably does not. Hence the reference of *the train* or *the bear* would not be clear to the listener even though the object is apparent.

This argument has some interest, but there is a difficulty for it with formally similar statements in which both the speaker and listener are aware of the class membership and the reference is still indefinite: such as the utterance 'It is, after all, only a *bear*', or 'The fact that it is *a bear* should not affect us.' In such cases it is no longer possible to argue that the speaker and listener share differing knowledge about the appropriateness of the reference for the nominated object; nevertheless the reference remains indefinite.

If nominal indefinite expressions fit into the categories of table 1.1, they probably do so as non-specific references. In the act of naming or attributing further characteristics to an object, a speaker is concerned only with placing the named object in its relationship to the rest of the members of the named class. In the instance above of a parent naming a bear for his child, he is not concerned with it as a particular bear, but only as a non-particular member of the class of bears. It is contrastively possible for nominal expressions to acquire specific status as members of their class. Some gain this unique status by virtue of definition, e.g. *'This is the biggest bear in the world'* (there is only one such bear). In other cases the situation may provide the context, for example 'One of these is a bear and the other is a raccoon. That one is *the bear.'* The possibility should not be overlooked, however, that nomination and attribution statements do not fall properly into the categories discussed above at all, though there is much overlap of meaning (cf. appendix xɪ for further discussion).

The conceptual basis for definite and indefinite reference

The general problem facing the child in making any semantic acquisition is a complex and difficult one. His task is to discover the proper situational uses of various phonological segments. His data for the task are the grammatical and semantic knowledge he may have of other sound segments used around the target segments and the non-linguistic context in which he hears all these segments used. In the particular case of articles the segments are phonologically slight ones, *a* (or *an* in front of words beginning with vowels, as in *an elephant*) and *the*. Their meanings are abstruse. They refer to no particular object, class of objects, or class of actions, as do, e.g. *mommy, dog,* or *push,* or even a consistent internal feeling such as is nominated by *want.* Their meaning inheres in the semantically abstract notions of specificity of reference and the specificity of a reference for their listener. Each of these presents what abstractly seem like severe problems of conceptualization. We shall consider each of the conceptual bases for definite—indefinite reference in turn to attempt greater insight into the child's problem.

Understanding classes and class membership

Underlying the system of specificity is the abstract system of classes, class membership, the relation of class members to other class members as well as simply the notion of any class member. The underlying basis for specificity cannot be found in particular objects or external physical attributes. A specific reference rests on the cognitive notion of unique member of a class. A specific reference is a reference to some member of the class nominated which has all the attributes required to be a member of that class plus others which make it distinctive. In situations where the referent is physically present such distinctive properties may be perceptual ones. Each object has its particular individual physical characteristics, and a certain individuality attained by the occupation of a unique spatio-temporal segment. Referents introduced to the speaker only verbally, however, have as distinctive properties only the propositional context in which they were introduced. When a speaker hears someone say 'I was walking down the street and a dog growled at me', the speaker has access to *dog* as a specific one only through the information 'growled at X when X was walking down the street'. Such discourse referents may furthermore be even more abstract in nature, both short-lived and highly hypothetical. In the cases discussed so far, expressions such as *the dog* have referred to a real dog unique in the class of dogs. But discourse referents may be introduced only hypothetically, in statements such as 'I wish we had *a dog* and *a ball* (non-specific references). We could throw *the ball* to *the dog* (specific references).' Referents hypothetically introduced in this manner exist only in the hypothetical mode of the discourse. It would be peculiar to continue afterwards 'Let's see how big the dog is', or 'I wonder where the dog is.'

Non-specific reference contrastively rests on the idea of any member of a class. The class member may be presumed to be existent, as when a speaker says 'I'd like to take out a book' at the library. Its existence may be only variably prospective, as in 'Let's buy a car', or 'Let's have a baby.' Or only the bare notion of any class member at all may remain, as in references to no member at all, e.g. 'I can't drive a car.'

The child must not have only developed awareness of such differences in types of class members and class membership. For use in the linguistic system he must operate recursively on his own awareness and monitor it for use in the verbal system. This is of course true for any instance of verbal expression. But here the cognitive dimension operated on seems peculiarly abstract, defined neither on particular perceptions or classes of perceptions, either external or internal.

The hopes for children's early acquisition of the ability to operate consistently with such a semantic system should be dim. Piaget in fact concluded (1962) that children between the ages of two and four have great difficulties with formulating the relations between individual class members and the generic notion of the class:

> We find one constant characteristic of the 'preconcepts' of this age which seems to be decisive. The child at this state achieves neither true generality nor true individuality, the notions he uses fluctuating incessantly between the two extremes (Piaget, 1962, p. 224).

Piaget produced a famous observation of his daughter Jacqueline, aged two and a half (2;6) at the time to support his claim:

> But also at 2;6 she used the term 'the slug' for the slugs we went to see every morning along a certain road. At 2;7,2 she cried: 'There it is' on seeing one, and when she saw another ten yards further on she said: 'There's the slug again.' I answered: 'But isn't it another one?' J. went back to see the first one. 'Is it the same one? – *Yes* – another slug? – *Yes* – Another or the same? – . . .?' The question obviously had no meaning for J (p. 225).

He cites a similar observation of Jacqueline at 3;3:

> J. was playing with a red insect, which disappeared. A quarter of an hour later when we were out for a walk we tried to look at a lizard, which darted away. Ten minutes afterwards we found another red insect. '*It's the red animal again*' (Piaget, 1962, p. 225).

These and other observations convinced Piaget that the young child does not differentiate individual members of a class clearly from one another, nor from the general class to which they belong. Interestingly, Piaget's evidence is essentially verbal, the form of the child's answer compared to the context. The observations are not always convincing. Jacqueline at 2;6 may have thought that slugs can travel very fast, and so believed that she was seeing the same slug again. Her comment at 3;3 seems even more reasonable in this light. But they are suggestive observations nonetheless; they imply either the more serious cognitive difficulties with the notions of class membership that Piaget believes them to, or problems with translating correct awareness into consistent and correct verbal usage.

Other work also suggests that the cognitive dimensions presupposed by specific and non-specific reference may give problems to the young child. Bruner *et al.* (1966) hold that the cognitive competence of the preschool child is limited in a serious way by the child's greater dependence on iconic representation, the use of perceptual imagery to represent the world. Imagic representation seems peculiarly ill-suited for representation of the difference between particular and non-particular, individual and general. Should a child translate expressions like *a dog* as used in 'I don't want *a dog*' or 'Let's get *a dog*' into imagic terms alone, he would have nothing but problems in distinguishing this non-particular dog from individual, particular dogs. Mature referential ability cannot depend heavily on iconic representation. If the young child's representations are heavily laden with imagery and only lightly based on amodal, abstract representations, the conceptual basis underlying specific and non-specific reference can only cause difficulty.

Taking the listener's point of view

Logically speaking, if the difficulties the child can be imagined to encounter with specificity are great, those he should encounter with taking into account his listener's knowledge are even greater. The child's difficult task is to learn that saying *the* X of something corresponds not only to his having clearly in mind a perhaps temporarily unique member of the class of Xs. His reference must also find in his listener an instantaneous recognition of a particular X unique from all other Xs in the context of the discourse. The speaker must be able to identify the X as one already conspicuous in the discourse either through unique physical presence, social knowledge, implication, or overt mention. Thus the child must both discover this condition on the use of *the* X from his own experiences and must discover as well the circumstances under which his listener will be able to make the requisite interpretation. For particular cases this knowledge may never stop growing, for it includes knowledge of matters such as a car's having an engine, all literary works having an end (*the end* of the book), and more particularly, a growing list of referents likely to be variously unique for friends, members of the family, members of social groups that he joins, and other kinds of non-linguistic knowledge that must interact with the linguistic knowledge of the general principles guiding the use of definite reference.

Children as egocentric communicators

Until recently, the picture available from developmental investigations of the child's ability to take into account the knowledge of his listener was one of little competence indeed. Piaget (1955) once again has provided seminal investigations. He asked children to tell complicated fairy tales and myths to still other children, and to explain to other children the workings of a mechanical tap or of a syringe. Questioning by the experimenters ascertained that the children understood the stories and tools they were to explain. But as explainers the children give poorly ordered, referentially careless accounts to their peer listeners. Piaget notes

> the explainer always gave us the impression of talking to himself, without bothering about the other child. Very rarely did he succeed in placing himself at the latter's point of view (Piaget, p. 115).

In particular, Piaget wrote that 'pronouns, personal and demonstrative adjectives, etc., "he, she", or "that, the, him", etc., are used right and left, without any indication of what they refer to. The other person is supposed to understand.' Piaget gives one child's account as a vivid example:

> Gio (8 years old) tells the story of Niobe in the role of explainer:
> *'Once upon a time there was a lady who has twelve boys and twelve girls, and then a fairy a boy and a girl. And then Niobe wanted to have some more sons* [than the fairy. Gio means by this that Niobe competed with the fairy, as was told in the text. But it will be seen how elliptical is his way of expressing it.] *Then she* [who?] *was angry. She* [who?] *fastened her* [how?] *to a stone.'* (Piaget, p. 116).

Work after Piaget's has initially confirmed his description of children's limited communication abilities. Second-grade children proved to explain a game no differently to a listener who could not see than to one who could in one study of many by Flavell *et al.* (1968).

Krauss and Glucksberg (1969) undertook a series of studies in which children of different ages were to communicate across a visual barrier which of a set of nonsense figures they were looking at. Preschool and young grammar school children were often very poor communicators indeed. Their descriptions were often ill-suited to give their listeners the information they needed to distinguish one figure from another, and ranged to the classically egocentric: one child described a form as 'a daddy's shirt' and described the next as 'another daddy's shirt'.

Non-egocentric communicative abilities in preschoolers

These general findings now find a counterpart, however, in a newer body of work that indicates children may not ignore their listeners' needs as blithely as we had thought. Shatz and Gelman (1973) asked four-year-old children to play with, in turn, adults and two-year-old children, using similar play materials with both the younger and older age groups. The four-year-olds turned out to talk differently to the younger two-year-olds than to adults in a number of important ways. They used more attention-getting verbal exclamations like 'Hey!' Their syntax was simpler, and contained a lower proportion of complex constructions such as embedded sentences. Maratsos (1973) had pre-school children play a very simple game in which they asked an adult experimenter for toys to put in a car. Even three-year-old children gave far more verbally explicit descriptions to an adult with eyes covered than to an adult who could see. More recently, Peterson (1974) has had children go back to the scene of some interesting incidents – a guinea pig escaped from a cage, some kool-aid spilled, a lost coat found – with either an adult who had been there at the time or an adult who had not been witness to the many incidents. The children talked differently to the unknowledgeable adult in a number of ways. They talked far more, and their descriptions of events were fuller and richer. Though full of many errors and inadequate descriptions, their narratives definitely showed in inclination to modulate their accounts according to the knowledgeability of their listeners.

It has become apparent, then, that what children know about communicating to others is simpler than what an adult knows, but they are not without some initial skills. The question is no longer whether children are egocentric. That question, I think, has become too general. The question is what kind of knowledge they have, in particular, how they may or may not apply that knowledge to the intricacies of formulating and using a particular semantic system, that of definite and indefinite reference, a system that requires the use of knowledge about others' referential knowledge in a systematic and abstract fashion.

2

Studying the acquisition of articles

Naturalistic work

We should like to know, naturally, a great deal about the acquisition of any semantic system, particularly one with the complex semantic and cognitive bases of articles. There are always more questions to ask than can be addressed directly or fully, but some of these are amenable to relatively rapid formulation and investigation. Such easier questions include the relatively simple one of the age at which a form becomes a stable one in the child's repertory. Following this determination we may ask more intricate questions, particularly questions of the accuracy of the child's initial formulations. Does the child's meaning resemble the adult's meaning? Does it contain some though not all of the mature meaning? Or is it founded on a systematically different basis, though appropriate in its effect in a number of cases? Such information tells us much about what the child acquires from contextual observation, and about how exact an analysis of the form he requires before instantiating his analysis in actual use.

It seems clear, and increasingly so, that the richest initial source of data for estimating children's knowledge may be found in recordings of their spontaneous productions in natural settings such as the home (Bloom *et al.*, 1974; Brown, 1973). Eventually we shall discuss the use of experiments, as is only appropriate in a book largely devoted to the exposition of experimental results. But naturalistic data offer a richness of sampling of contexts and use that experimental investigations cannot approach.

The articles provide examples of forms that may profitably be observed naturalistically. Particularly in the study of the development of word meanings, this is not always so. Unlike basic syntactic constructions, individual words may occur only infrequently in speech samples. Even rather basic lexical items such as *front* and *back* or *know* or *more* and *less* may occur with extremely low frequency in spontaneous speech. The first uses discovered in samples may fall well after the child has begun to understand and use the items, for the same reason that an adult's understanding of words such as *astronomy* is represented only poorly in his speech. Some forms, however, occur quite commonly in speech, even obligatorily so. Brown (1973) has with a group of associated investigators (Bellugi, 1967; Brown and Bellugi, 1964; Brown, Cazden, and Bellugi, 1968; Brown and Hanlon, 1970; Cromer, 1968) gathered longitudinal, naturalistic recordings of the speech of three children who have become well known in the literature of language acquisition as Adam, Eve, and Sarah. Among the problems studied (Brown, 1973) has been the children's acquisition of fourteen very commonly used grammatical morphemes such as *in*, *on*, the progressive ending *-ing*, the past tense *-ed* and conveniently, the articles *a* and *the*.

The age of acquisition

For each of these morphemes Brown (also cf. Cazden, 1968) has defined a point of stable acquisition. By various criteria it can be judged for various morphemes whether or not the morpheme should appear in a context. Some cases are simple. The definite article *the* must appear before some terms, e.g. in a frame such as 'This is ——— middle one', or before the word *same*, e.g. 'I saw ——— same one.' In other cases a combination of grammatical context and situational context determines an obligation to use one of the articles. Acquisition of a morpheme is said to take place when the morpheme has appeared in its obligatory contexts at least 90 per cent of the time in three consecutive speech samples. In chronological terms, using these criteria, stable usage of the articles appeared for the three children studied between an estimated thirty-two months (for Eve, the generally fastest child) and forty-one months of age (Sarah, generally the slowest child).

Estimating competence from the naturalistic data

It would be remarkable for children to command the full semantics of definite and indefinite articles at around three years of age, but information about the stability of use cannot by itself provide the information necessary to draw this conclusion. Brown also attempted an estimation of the semantic appropriateness of the children's usage, drawing on samples of the children's speech around the time of stable acquisition, and comparing the use of the article with the verbal and non-verbal context of its use. With such data he judged the appropriateness of the child's use where possible, although there were a good many doubtful cases.

Specificity and non-specificity

For those instances in which the child's point of view converged with his listener's, successful references very largely outnumbered the unsuccessful. A large number of references specific for neither speaker or listener were successfully made. Examples included 'Put *a band-aid* on it' (Eve), 'This don't have *a wheel* on it', and 'Make *a B*' (Sarah). No example was found of a child erroneously referring definitely to non-unique or non-existent class members. Despite the abstractness of this category, the three children seemed to have good knowledge of its use by the time they were using articles stably. They also displayed many correct uses of references specific for both speaker and listener alike. References included those unique for all (*the sky, the ground*), unique in a given setting (*the floor, the couch, the ceiling*), salient for a social group (*the mailman, the TV, the subway*) and definite reference to other physically conspicuous unique objects. Definite references were also found which were specified by entailment (*the driver's wheel, the motor* (of a train), *the nose, the nurse* (at a doctor's office), parts of a family (*the grandma*), and of a band-aid (*the sticky of the bandage*); by definition ('That's *the middle*', *the next page*); and specified by prior utterance ('That *a jeep*. I put some in *the jeep*'). There were also errors, especially in the categories of entailment (e.g. 'Where there's *a heel*?' said of a particular sock; *a chin*, in naming features of a face) and in references specified by prior utterance (e.g. 'I never drop *a watch*', said of an already specified watch; '*a jeep* is coming', of an already mentioned jeep). Brown suggests, however, that

> there are far too many correct unimitated instances of both categories of reference to suppose that the children did not know that when a whole entailed one of a certain part the article should be *the* and that when a reference is repeated the article should be *the* (p. 35).

The occurring errors are ascribed to children's possible lack of knowledge of part-whole assemblages in the case of entailment, and occasional failure to keep track of previously specified references rather than general ignorance in the failure of definite reference to previously referred to objects. The children's early usage, then, apparently displays considerable knowledge of the semantic factor of specificity vs non-specificity.

Competence with divergence of viewpoints

The case is different for instances in which the child and his listener's knowledge did not converge. Instances were infrequent when the child made indefinite reference to objects for which reference was specific for the child but not his listener. Many of the instances in this category appear to be types of naming statements, such as 'He's *a witch*' (Adam) and 'It's *a gun*.' In contrast, the transcripts showed many apparently erroneous definite references made by the child when the reference was specific only for himself. A convincing sign of the erroneousness of the reference in many exchanges was the puzzled or interrogative response of the mother. Two such exchanges were quoted earlier in this book:

> Sarah: *The cat's* dead.
> Mother: What cat?
>
> Adam: Put it up, *the man* says.
> Mother: Who's the man?

Such replies show the failure of the reference to be uniquely identifiable for the listener quite directly. In other cases the reply may display the problem in a more subtle fashion. Eve, for example, once asked 'Where's *the stool*?' apparently having one in mind, and her mother replied 'There's one over here', showing that the reference to *stool* did not elicit knowledge in her mother of a particular stool Eve intended to refer to. In this category, then, children's erroneous definite references were far more frequent than correct indefinite ones. Children's expected failure to take into account the point of view of the other finds substantiation in these instances.

Summary of the evidence

By the time of stable acquisition, then, naturalistic evidence indicates that children learning the use of articles have differentiated the dimension of specific vs non-specific reference with some precision, apparently contrary to Piaget's earlier assertions that children of this age cannot cope successfully with the relevant conceptual bases of the linguistic distinctions. But they do not appear to be able to take into account those cases in which their own knowledge diverges from that of their listener, and so refer specifically and non-specifically for themselves, i.e. egocentrically.

These seem reasonable conclusions based on a rich sample of observational data. Nevertheless the present book comprises a series of experimental investigation largely of young children's competence in dealing with articles, with some emphasis on evaluating the competence of children who have had their use only for a short interval. An inevitable question is 'why this book?' I shall try to give an answer in the succeeding section on both broad and narrow theoretical grounds. In the process I shall be attempting to justify an assertion that there remain important aspects of the young child's competence in using definite and indefinite reference regarding which the 'naturalistic data permit no conclusions at all' (Brown, 1973, p. 355), as well as attempting to bring up more general problems concerning the evaluation of competence.

Problems in evaluating semantic competence
Specific and non-specific reference: instantiating general competence

In the past years we have grown accustomed to attributing complex and abstract syntactic and semantic capacities to children and adults in describing the acquisition and command of human language systems. It has become a truism that the individual behaviors or even classes of behaviors we exhibit in speaking are not as general as the knowledge that underlies them. A speaker's knowledge encompasses a set of rules and concepts more abstract and more broad than any particular instantiation of that competence in actual behavior.

Yet it remains a fact that our only means of evaluating and inferring abstract concepts in the knowledge of an adult or a child is through particular instances of behavior, whether they be judgements and intuitions in adults, or actual records of speech performance in children, or performance in experimentally arranged situations. Sometimes the data are so striking that the inference becomes an obvious one. When we see children using the regular past tense in reasonable but inappropriate forms such as *breaked* or *goed*, it becomes clear that they have done more than memorize individual past tenses when they say *pushed* or *kicked*. But in other cases the data are not as clear or obvious, and the processes of inference become more difficult. It remains a familiar danger in the evaluation of what children know that we might attribute to them knowledge more abstract, generalized, and unified than they actually have because they command part of the appropriate system. If we tend to assume that the system being learned is indeed homogeneous, then demonstration of competence in one aspect is a good sign of complete competence.

But we know this is not always the case. In the acquisition of syntax, children acquire the use of the negative words *can't* and *don't* before showing any use of the positive auxiliaries *can* and *do*. As a result we infer that *can't* and *don't* are not part of an integrated auxiliary and negation system, even though their limited use is quite correct (Bellugi, 1967). The same difficulty arises with the evaluation of semantic competence. The child's initial semantic concept may be exact in the uses we see, but in fact neither be as general in extent or as unified as the abstract concept that would be appropriate to describe the adult's behavior in the same instances, if it is even appropriate for the adult. What appears to be a general competence may be a more limited series of particular competencies.

The abstractness of reference
The naturalistic evidence Brown reports seems to support a very general knowledge on children's parts of the abstract semantics which form the basis of the dimension of specific and non-specific reference. But on inspection, most of the evidence for specific and definite reference occurs in the case of reference to objects and people directly in visible sight, particularly for categories such as reference made specific by a previous reference. In some cases there are definite references to non-visible referents, such as *the subway* or *the sun*. But such cases could easily be ones where the article is a routine-like part of the expression for the child, just as *the* in *the Hague*, or *the same* is for adults. Most of the non-specific references, on the other hand, occur when no particular object is in sight, e.g. 'This don't have *a wheel* on it.' The child's apparently general competence could be an amalgam of particular learned definite and indefinite references combined with a distinction largely commanded by visibility and non-visibility.

Aside from these more extreme possibilities, there exist more subtle ones. Knowledge of the semantic usage might be correct in familiar situations but nevertheless quite limited. Consider the continuum of the concreteness of our knowledge of referents. At one end of this continuum are those instances in which a particular referent is physically present. These correspond most often to clearly non-routine-like definite uses in the naturalistic data. The referent is unique by virtue of its being outstanding in a situation which forms the present context for the speaker.

More abstractly we come to a situation where the speaker has had direct experience with the referent but it is no longer present. He might recall an animal he saw the day before. This type of knowledge is more abstract than the first. Means of mental storage of the referent must now be employed, and the referent distinguished as a unique class member solely on the basis of internal evidence. Recall the observations which led Piaget to his conclusion about the young child's inability to distinguish particular class members from general class membership. They were of this kind, where an animal or insect had been seen before and another was seen.

Both of the above situations, despite the greater abstractness of the second, have in common that they entail knowledge by acquaintance (Russell, 1920). In each case the speaker knows the referent through his own personal experience. Other referents are known, in Russell's terminology, by description only. Such is our knowledge of most historical figures and many geographical locations. They are described to us, but never experienced directly. Similarly, some referents may become particular for us only by verbal description. Only a propositional context makes them unique and so entails specific reference to them. At perhaps the most abstract end of the continuum are referents introduced only fictionally or hypothetically, as in 'If Bartok had written a symphony and a flute concerto, *the symphony* would have been more interesting.' The referents of the appropriate definite expressions, though they may be described and discussed at length, exist only as imaginary constructs and cannot be 'known' in a real sense. The mental entries employed for them are of an abstract and short-lived nature indeed.

The mature system of adult specific reference apparently treats these different kinds of particular referents as semantically equivalent. But the naturalistic evidence only weakly supports the notion that children initially command such a general and abstract range of usage. Indeed it is no doubt observations of children's failures in the more abstract, less concrete referential situations that formed the basis for Piaget's low estimate of the young child's referential powers.

A first purpose of the experimentation that will be reported in the succeeding chapters, then, is an estimate of the generality and abstractness of children's early stable use of specific and non-specific reference. Can they extend their understanding to situations in which both specific reference and non-specific reference are entailed only by verbal contexts? Can they employ the difference between the two in novel contexts unlikely to have been learned in familiar contexts? Our question is the generality of the semantic formulations children build on the basis of somewhat limited initial experience. We shall find, in fact, that their competence is indeed highly abstract and general; though slightly more fragile and open to the interruption of cognitive difficulties and the use of routine-like responses than children who have had use of the system for a longer period, the competence of children who have not had long use of the articles includes knowledge of the speciffc — non-specific semantic dimension in a wide variety of novel contexts, some completely verbal. Correspondingly the evidence to be discussed opposes Piaget's evaluation of children's means of storage for class members and class membership, showing their cognitive abilities in this respect to be more advanced than appears to be the case in his (and Bruner's) description.

Non-egocentric reference

The evidence Brown cites suggests, not surprisingly, that young children frequently fail in their initial use of articles to distinguish between those occasions in which their listener's knowledge converges with their own and those in which it does not. Adam, Eve, and Sarah's definite references frequently failed to elicit recognition of the intended referent in their listeners, and instances of introductory, specific indefinite references were few and limited. In Piaget's terminology, such children fail to 'decenter' from their own viewpoint in their use of articles, and so are egocentric. But such an 'explanation', I think, errs in a fundamental theoretical direction, and brings up a general problem that deserves exposition here, for it is relevant to other aspects of the experimental results to be explicated.

General problems of estimating non-uniform competence

Much of our study of children's development in general is taken up with a question which may be phrased 'Does the child have it yet?' where 'it' may stand for some competence, knowledge, rule or operation. Often underlying such study is the assumption that the investigated competence is relatively homogeneous and general; we assume that we can test for its presence by the use of any number of different instantiating operations or observations.

Such an assumption, it has become increasingly clear, fails on a number of grounds. The chief failings, it seems to me, fall into two major categories: I shall call them *level of competence* and *unity of competence*. The difficulty with level of competence problems is that the same competence may be understood and employed at a number of different levels. Consider the case of knowledge of the rules of English word order. The knowledge speakers have enables them to judge as anomalous sentences such as *Mary John likes* or *Likes Mary John*. Adults generally obey such rules in their spontaneous speech, and can give sophisticated judgements of the acceptability of English and non-English word strings. Some may even be able to verbalize their knowledge more abstractly, noting that in English the proper word order for simple sentences is subject—verb—object. Unlike adults, children cannot give clear judgements of acceptability of sentences for some time, even at times when their spontaneous speech shows convincingly that they implicitly obey such rules firmly (DeVilliers and DeVilliers, 1974).

In a similar instance, adults seem to have a rather general knowledge of the word classes of English, such as verb, adjective, noun, and prepositions. In the familiar association tests, in which the subject is asked to give a word in association to a stimulus, their associations tend to be in the same word class. E.g. an association to 'dog' might be 'cat' or 'animal'. If we ask adults to put together words into piles based on their meaning similarities, they put nouns with nouns, verbs with verbs, and so on (Anglin, 1970). Again they may even show conscious verbal knowledge of the word classification of various words.

Children, contrastively, fail to show such abstract knowledge. In association tests their associations are likely to be of different word classes, e.g. 'bark' to 'dog'. In clustering tasks, they far less frequently cluster together words of the same form class. But once again their spontaneous speech displays their knowledge. Failures to employ word classes properly, resulting in anomalies such as 'This greens' or 'I just ideaed something' are extremely rare.

In these instances, the children's spontaneous behaviors provide convincing evidence that they control the abstract syntactic systems of interest, and only lack the ability to generalize this knowledge to tasks such as word associations, word clustering, or grammaticality judgements. For adults a number of tests may successfully tap the same competence. But the resulting assumption that any test of competence is as satisfactory as another breaks down because the competence is not used homogeneously at all levels.

At least one of the difficulties with diagnosing egocentrism, in contrast, seems to be that of (lack of) unity of competence. Egocentric behavior is frequently treated as though it were the result of a unitary state, with a single cause and consistent exemplifications, something like measles and its symptoms. We tend to think that someone is egocentric or is not egocentric. What is taken to be a homogeneous competence, however, almost surely is not. It is doubtful that there is any single competence to test at all, hence the problem is that a false unity of competence is assumed.

For a while, as discussed earlier, it did seem quite plausible that preschool and young children were rather uniformly egocentric, while adults largely were not. Preschool children, unlike adults, could not consciously verbalize a need to take into account the viewpoint of the other. They correspondingly almost invariably failed as communicators to take into account divergent viewpoints, at least in the tasks studies (Piaget, 1955; Flavell *et al.*, 1968; Krauss and Glucksberg, 1969). Nor is it to be denied that their failures were sometimes impressive. Krauss and Glucksberg report, for example, the following exchange in one of their tasks, in which one child is to try to communicate to another which of six nonsense forms he is looking at, across a vision-blocking screen:

> First child: It's this one.
> Second child: This one?
> First child: No.

But lately even preschool children have been shown to have some ability to adjust their communications to make them successful ones, either by generally useful attention-getting devices or by actual changes in the verbal content of their communications that is appropriate to the task (Maratsos, 1973; Mueller, 1972; Shatz & Gelman, 1973; Peterson, 1974). They also have shown simple but definite abilities to make judgements of others' differing visual perceptions (Masangkay, *et al.*,

1974; Lempers *et al.*, 1974). The matrix of results has become a mixed one. It is no longer meaningful to say that younger children are ego-centric, or fail to decenter to the viewpoint of others, as though this were a central, unitary condition, though they may fail more often than adults.

At least some of the reasons for this are easy to see. Consider in particular the case of using definite and indefinite articles. A child could be often sensitive to the need to adjust communications to others, whatever the level of abstractness or generality of this knowledge, resulting in successful communication in a number of tasks. He might describe events more fully when necessary or useful, or point out objects to communicate more clearly. Yet in formulating the particular seman-tics of definite and indefinite articles, he might, judging from the contexts of use around him, fail to see the relevance of judging his listener's viewpoint. His definitions for articles would correspondingly be egocentric in the face of non-egocentric behavior elsewhere because he had not noticed the relevance of communication adjustment to using articles in particular. It becomes obvious that we err in seeking to characterize such a child uniformly as 'egocentric' or not 'ego-centric'.

Besides the problem of generality of competence, though, there is an issue remaining of whether or not children have, somehow, knowl-edge stored at some level that sometimes one needs to adjust com-munications to be more informative to a listener. The situations in which preschool children's competence has emerged significantly have tended to be simpler tasks than those formerly used, and often naturalistic or closer to naturalistic ones. It becomes difficult to tell if the child has abstracted a general notion of communication which frequently fails because of particular task difficulties, or whether his successes stem from particular learned communicative adjustments which are not mediated by more general nonegocentric principles. Later (chapter 8) we shall be able to analyze these difficulties with greater particularity.

In fact, the experimental results we obtain will display that the problems of diagnosis of non-egocentric competence remain quite severe even when confined to as small a realm as the use of articles. Our results will confirm, or at least support, the proposition that children's initial use of articles often fails to be non-egocentric. In fact, even children who have used articles for some time have continued varied difficulties in their non-egocentric use. Although skill in employing articles non-egocentrically improves, we shall find that unlike the case for specificity of reference, it is more difficult to mark the acquisition of a single, apparently more unified non-egocentric competence. In fact, we shall even find weaknesses in the discourse competence of adult speakers, weaknesses difficult to distinguish in kind from the more widespread difficulties of younger children. The chief outcome, then, may be seen to be an opportunity to dissect the problems of diagnosis with far greater exactness, a greater familiarity with the difficulties of showing an 'it' that is acquired, if 'it' is the appropriate grouping of competence at all.

The use and perils of experiments

Finally, a last focus of succeeding investigations will be the experiments reported on in the succeeding chapters. Experiments derive both benefit and loss in their distance from naturalistic situations. The benefits are clear. Naturalistic samples may fail in various ways to give us the information necessary to resolve interpretation problems. A behavior of interest may be completely lacking, and we do not know whether its absence is caused by sampling difficulties or a real lack of the requisite competence. A feature of the transcripts of two- and three-year-olds, for example, is the absence of much discourse about situations and referents not in the immediate or near immediate context. Yet as we saw, information about children's competence in dealing with such situations is crucially needed to complete an estimate of their powers to make reference. The need for this kind of supplementary information provided the major motivation for carrying out the studies reported in the present work.

But it is unquestionable that experiments also provide their own difficulties of interpretation, especially when compared with naturalistic data (Bloom, 1974; Brown, 1973; Fernald, 1972). A constant difficulty in working with younger children is maintaining their interest and compliance. When a child speaks in natural surroundings he is probably interested in what he is saying, or he would generally choose not to speak at all. In experimental contexts this minimal level of attention cannot be assumed. We ask the subject to attend and comply largely at our convenience, and we may ask when the child is not interested or fully attentive. The chief resultant danger is underestimating the child's competence. Related dangers may be found in possible shyness of the child, or his not being accustomed to the experimental surroundings, each of which may distract him from attending to the procedures as we would like.

A second and more abstruse kind of experimental peril lies in the fact that we can only engage abstract competence through a number of intervening behaviors and operations (Flavell and Wohlwill, 1969). In one of the studies to be reported, for example, the child is asked to attend to stories of some complexity and then give an answer to a question about the story. It is a necessary prerequisite to answering correctly that much information about the story context and the referents of the story be held in mind as the child answers. We shall be able to show that variables such as the form of questioning and the memory requirements of the task affect the experimental outcomes in systematic though not *a priori* predictable ways. Such methodological analyses of the interaction of the test employed with the competence to be tested form another of the central concerns of this work.

3

A brief introduction to the design and procedures

Nature and procurement of subjects

The data discussed by Brown suggest that the use of definite and indefinite articles becomes stable sometime in the period of about two and a half through three and a half years of age. In the study to be described, two groups of children were seen in experimental settings. The younger group was a group estimated not to have had the use of articles for very long. They ranged in age from 32 through 42 months, with a median age of 39 months. All but two of the children ranged in age from 36 through 42 months of age, i.e. three through three and a half years, the two exceptions being 32 and 35 months. For the sake of convenience I shall refer to this younger group throughout the book as three-year olds, although the age range 43 through 47 months was not investigated. The older group ranged in age from 48 through 59 months, with a median age of 55 months, and will be referred to as the four-year-old group throughout. Each group was comprised of twenty children, ten boys and ten girls.

The subjects were solicited by means of newspaper advertisements in the *Harvard Crimson* and the *Harvard Independent* and various local small papers such as *The Brookline Citizen*. The sample was overwhelmingly middle-class in background.

General procedure

Each child was seen three times. The first session consisted of a visit to the child's home. A primary purpose of the home visits was to be certain that the three-year-old children seen experimentally actually had stable use of the articles. Children who did not appear to have demonstrable spontaneous use of articles were not seen further, since our interests were not primarily normative. Five of the three-year-olds visited did not show spontaneous use, four boys and one girl. Interestingly, one four-year-old girl also turned out not to use articles at all in her speech, though obviously quite advanced in her speech in other ways. The visit at the home also had two other purposes. The first of these was to be certain that the child was not too shy to talk fairly easily to the experimenter, or that he did not otherwise take offense. The second was to ensure that the experimenter was a familiar figure when the child participated in the later experimental sessions, which were not at the home. Toys were taken to the home to play with, but no experimental testing was undertaken. Both three- and four-year-olds were visited in the same way.

The occurrence of the second and third sessions was contingent on the outcome of the home visit. Aside from the five three-year-olds and one four-year-old not seen because of their lacking the use of articles, one four-year-old boy was not seen because he showed an unaccountable aversion for me, hiding under a couch as soon as I entered the house. All experimental investigation took place in these later two sessions, spaced approximately one week apart and beginning one week after the home visit. These sessions took place at William James Hall, not at the home. Pilot work seemed to indicate that children were more attentive in the unfamiliar setting than at home, particularly since the experimental sessions could last as long as an hour, depending on the child. Bringing children directly to the experimental settings without a home visit appeared to result in a good amount of shyness and nervousness; at least this was my impression from pilot work. The combination of a home visit for familiarity with the experimenter and actually participating in the experimental sessions at an unfamiliar though friendly looking place seemed to result in an optimal mixture of familiarity and respect. Both experimental sessions were recorded completely with an Uher 4000 L portable tape recorder.

An introduction to the overall experimental design

Children were assessed experimentally for a number of competencies in the comprehension and productive use of definite and indefinite articles. I shall list below the names of the different types of the tasks that were employed with a very brief description of each. In later chapters the procedures will be described far more exactly, with the results and discussion appropriate to each. The tasks employed were as follows:

(1) Comprehension tests. Three stories told to the child which he acted out with toys.
(2) Stories. Thirteen stories which the child heard and had to complete. No toys or pictures were present to refer to.
(3) Imitations with expansions. This task was given to three-year-olds only. The child imitated sentences which formed a complete, very short story. At crucial points an appropriate article was left out of the story for the child to supply, it was hoped, in his imitations.
(4) Games. Two games played twice by each child. In these games he had to ask for toys one at a time out of variously arranged arrays of toys.
(5) Assessment imitations. At the end of testing, each child received a set of fourteen sentences varying in complexity to imitate. The child's ability to imitate these sentences formed an index of his linguistic competence besides age.

Except possibly for the comprehension tests, it would not have been possible to give most of the children all of the tests in any of the categories at once. The thirteen stories, told without accompanying toys, were especially difficult in this respect. The tasks were therefore divided as evenly as possible through the two experimental sessions for each child. Each task was given a certain number of times over the two sessions to each child, as listed below:

(1) Comprehension tests: 3 periods of testing.
(2) Stories: 4 periods.
(3) Imitations with expansions: 1 period.
(4) Games: 4 periods.

In the division of the task periods throughout the two experimental sessions a number of goals were primary. Each task period of a certain type (e.g. Stories) was placed as far as possible from the previous period of identical test type. Two dominant orders for a single session were made up for this purpose. Order 1: Stories — Comprehension — Games — Stories — Comprehension — Games. Order 2: Stories — Games — Comprehension — Stories — Games — Comprehension. A child receiv-Order 1 in the first experimental sessions received Order 2 in the second, and vice versa. Each session always began with a Stories period. In pilot work Stories were found to be the least popular tasks; placed first, they were the earliest completed in each experimental session Because there were only three Comprehension periods as opposed to four each of Stories and Games periods, no two sessions were perfectly symmetrical for any child. Two overall designs for task presentation resulted from these considerations:

Design A

Session 1: Stories – Comprehension – Games – Stories – Comprehension – Games.

Session 2: Stories – Games – Comprehension – Stories – Games – Imitations.

Design B

Session 1: Stories – Games – Comprehension – Stories – Games – Comprehension.

Session 2: Stories – Comprehension – Games – Stories – Games – Imitations.

For the four-year-olds, Imitations included only the assessment set of fourteen imitations. Three-year-olds received both the assessment set and the Imitations with expansions set, with the assessment set given first.

Within each age group of twenty children, ten children each were assigned to Design A and ten to Design B. It can be reported here that no differences were found between these two groups.

These designs constitute the broad outlines within which the experimental tests were embedded. In the chapters which follow I shall devote one or two chapters to the description of each task, with its corresponding results and related discussion.

4
Tests of comprehension

A preliminary theoretical discussion

There are clear semantic differences between the expressions *a dog* and *the dog*. But how can a child's ability to comprehend such differences be investigated convincingly? One way is to create stories in which the difference between the articles carries an information load far greater than usual, but in which different outcomes should follow from understanding something of the difference between specific and nonspecific reference.

The difference stems from the principle that discourse referents of the type discussed by Karttunen should be referred to by a definite reference in the discourse. When a discourse referent has already been established, an indefinite reference indicates that no particular member of the same class is being referred to, hence not the already conspicuous discourse referent. The difference can be seen in the sentences below.

(1) Harry saw a dog, and John saw *the dog* too.
(2) Harry saw a dog, and John saw *a dog* too.

In sentence number (1), the use of *the dog* makes it clear that the dog being mentioned is one already established as a discourse referent, hence the dog that Harry saw. In (2), the second reference to *a dog* implies that some other dog must be meant, or else the expression *the dog* would have been employed to make reference to the dog already conspicuous in the discourse. Before discussing the stories actually constructed to assess children's competence in understanding this delicate usage, however, I shall first discuss the possible determinants of the comprehension of definite and indefinite expressions.

Comprehension of definite expressions

Probably the best account of comprehension of definite expressions is that whenever a definite expression is used, the listener inspects the context of its use and searches for some member of the class nominated that is outstanding in the situation. It need not be a class already verbally mentioned. In the discussion of entailment we found that definite expressions may be employed without previous verbal mention (e.g. 'John was driving home, and *the car* broke down'). In physical contexts, a simple pointing may make the reference of a definite expression straightforward.

Thus, in the case of (1) above, when *the dog* is mentioned, there is already one particular dog conspicuous in the conversation – the one Harry saw. Interpretation of *the dog* to refer to that particular dog is straightforward. When inspection of a larger conversational segment is required, interpretation may be more laborious but is essentially quite simple:

> (3) Once there were two brothers, Tom and John. Tom brought a snake home one day, and put it in the family car. John then brought home a snake also, putting his under the living room couch. Shortly afterwards, their mother had to go to the supermarket. As was customary, she took the car. She was driving down the road, when suddenly *the snake* slithered out onto her lap and bit her.

The snake must refer to the snake Tom put in the car. Here it is interesting that in the discourse as a whole there are two snakes mentioned. In finding an interpretation for a definite expression, the speaker may have to narrow down to a more particular context of the discourse, one with material more pointedly about the referent of the definite expression.

Where contextual inspection gives no outstanding candidate as reference for the definite expression, interpretation is apparently impossible:

> (4) Mary saw Tom and Horace. *The boy* fell down.

The boy here is not even ambiguous; its use here is simply anomalous. The problem is that there is no reason to prefer one boy or the other as being the boy particularly likely to fall down. This is not a special problem with *Tom* and *Horace*, the possible reference for *the boy*, being in a conjunction:

(5) Once there were two brothers, John and Tom. John brought home a frog and set it on a chair in the living room. Tom then brought a frog home as well, and put it on the couch. After a while their mother came in with dinner. *The frog* jumped into the food.

Again the context provides no reason to prefer one frog or the other as the likelier reference of *the frog*.

The most recent referent theory of definite reference

All three of the last examples have interest as well in that they oppose a theory of definite reference which I shall call the *most recent referent theory*. According to this theory, a listener interprets definite references as referring to the member of the class that was last referred to. Such an hypothesis is based on simple cases such as (1), which I cite here again.

(1) Harry saw a dog, and John saw *the dog* too.

The listener finds the reference of *the dog* by inspecting the context for the last dog referred to, and here finds the dog introduced in the clause 'Harry saw a dog.' The reference of *the dog* is then taken to be the dog seen by Harry.

Consider now examples (3), (4), and (5). In (3), *the snake* refers unambiguously to the snake put in the car, which happens to have been the first of the two snakes introduced in the story, and so not the snake mentioned closest to the expression *the snake*. Possibly, of course, strong contextual effects may override the most recent referent interpretation method, making the example less damaging. But examples (4) and (5) are damaging, particularly (5). Here the method of inspecting the context for a plausibly unique reference gives no clear reference. But the most recent referent theory does make an assignment, since the frog brought home by Tom is introduced second, both narratively and chronologically. Yet the definite expression *the frog* fails to make interpretable reference.

Perhaps the effect of recency is very short-lived. In example (5) there is a certain amount of intervening material between the introduction of each of the frogs and the definite expression *the frog*. Test cases may be found in stories like the following, where distance between the more recent referent and the definite expression is small.

(6) Once there were two brothers, John and Tom. John brought home a squirrel. Then Tom also brought home a squirrel. *The squirrel* became restless and hopped on the floor.

To me and several others I have asked, *the squirrel* still fails to make reference, even with a referent quite close before it. Overall it seems that if there is any effect of recency by itself, the effect is extremely weak if not non-existent. The most likely theory of how definite expressions are interpreted appears to be the theory of contextual inspection for a conspicuous member. This is perhaps a rough and not very explicit theory, but I think it is essentially correct.

Comprehension of indefinites

We have seen that the general effect of an indefinite reference is to shift reference from a discourse referent,[1] an already conspicuous member of the nominated class. I cite example (2) once more to illustrate this effect.

(2) Harry saw a dog, and John saw *a dog* too.

There are two major possibilities to explain the shift of reference brought about by the use of an indefinite expression in this way. The first of these is what I shall call *negative inference*. The listener reasons, in effect, that the indefinite expression stands for any member of the class at all. An already conspicuous member of the nominated class hardly qualifies as 'any member of the class,' so a new member must be intended. A second possibility implies a more automatic processing, and I shall accordingly call it *automatic introduction of new referent*. One of the main functions of indefinites, particularly the specific indefinite expression, is to introduce new referents to a listener. Perhaps the listener automatically interprets the second indefinite expression as making reference to a different class member.

Listeners may quite conceivably use either method, and the grounds for distinguishing among them are slight. It seems to me that the negative inference explanation is the more nearly correct one. One observation is that the speaker may use a second indefinite expression in a manner such as to surprise his listener by having it refer to the referent of the first. Here is an example:

1. This generalization only applies in certain contexts. 'Commentary' indefinites as in 'It was nice to find *a squirrel*' do not shift reference in this way (cf. appendix XI D for further discussion), nor do naming statements such as 'The animal was *a squirrel*.'

(7) John saw a dog, and Harry saw a dog too. It was the same dog!

It is a weak joke, but it is possible. With strong reference shifting terms such as *another* the effect is impossible. Consider 'Harry saw a dog, and John saw another dog. It was the same dog!' The speaker does not seem to be joking, but very confused.

I also believe that the reference shifting effect becomes stronger as the first referent is introduced as a more conspicuous one. Actors are intuitively more conspicuous than those acted on. From this we might predict that someone introduced as an actor is less likely to be the referent of a second indefinite expression. Compare (8) and (9):

(8) There were three men. *A man* kissed Martha and then *a man* kissed Samantha.

(9) There were three men. Martha kissed *a man* and then Samantha kissed *a man*.

I would judge, though weakly, that the second instance of *a man* is more likely to refer to another man in example (8) than in (9). This follows if indefinites refer to 'any member' of the class, and an actor is less 'any member' than someone acted on, making the shift of reference more likely in (8). A few people I have asked informally agree with me concerning this judgement, but this naturally does not amount to a systematic sample, and the intuitions are very weak.

In any case, the reference-shifting effect of indefinite expressions allows us to see what competence children have in understanding definite and indefinite expressions, particularly in contexts where other expressions would be more appropriate, putting much weight on a good understanding of the semantic differences. We may also see whether the use of the system for a longer time leads to substantial changes in the nature of the competence shown by the children.

A description of the tasks

The stories

Children who took part in the study were asked to act out stories which I told to them. They were supplied with appropriate toys for the task, and explaining to them what was to be done was quite easy. Each story had two versions, one with an indefinite at a crucial point in the story, the other with a definite expression at the same point. Each child received only one version of any given story, either a definite or indefinite version.

Three stories were used, but there were five tests contained in the stories. A description of each story follows, with the testing alternatives given in brackets.

Story 1. *The Table Story.* The toys for this story were four wooden dogs, a wooden boy, a plastic table, and four plastic chairs. In this story the child was to handle the dogs and the chairs, while I began the story moving the boy around. Each child also set the chairs at the table. All of the toys were small enough to be handled easily by the children in the study. The boy and dog dolls were all Fisher Price dolls and were already familiar to many of the children.

After the preliminaries, the story was told to the child in the following way:

'Now this boy came and sat down in one of the chairs. And just as he sat down, suddenly {a, the} chair fell over.'

Here, of course, if the child hears *the chair*, he should tip over the same chair as the one the boy sat in. The contrastive response, to *a chair*, is to tip over another of the chairs. Something to note about the wording of the story, perhaps, is the use of *suddenly* in front of the crucial articles. This was done for two reasons. First, it draws attention to what is said immediately afterwards. More important, the end vowel of *suddenly* provides a good phonological environment in which the delicate sounds of the articles may be heard distinctively.

After the child has made his choice of chairs, and tipped over the boy's chair or another, everything is set right again, and the story continues:

'Now one of the dogs jumped onto the table. The boy looked at him, but he just barked, "woof, woof". And now {the, a} dog ran under the table.' (*Now* also provides a good phonological environment for clear hearing of the articles). The story ends with all of the dolls getting seated and doing pretty much whatever the child likes for a short interval.

Story 2. *Dogs and Cars (with one boy).* The toys used were four Fisher Price cars, a Fisher Price boat, a wooden boy doll, four wooden dog dolls, and a wooden hill. The hill was large enough so that the cars could go up and down with ease. The four cars and the boat were laid out in a line, with a dog beside each car. The children were cautioned not to put the dogs into the cars. (A majority of the children complained at this point that another dog was needed for the boat.) In this story I moved the boy doll once more. The story the children heard began as follows:

'One of the dogs got into a car. He drove up the hill and he drove down again. Then he came back. Good. Now {he, one} got into the boat.'

This test constitutes the only assessment in all of these studies of children's understanding of definite and indefinite reference not exemplified in the articles *a* and *the*. *He* and *one* are pronouns. *He* is a definite pronoun. It refers to a specific member of the class of masculine referents. *One* is an indefinite that refers to any member of an already known class. (*He* has feminine and neuter contrasts in *she* and *it* in the nominative, for example, while *one* can stand for any gender.) The semantic use is clear, nevertheless, and corresponds to the general definite–indefinite split. For *he* the child should select the same dog to get into the boat, while for *one* another dog should be selected.

After this point in the story, there is some impromptu exposition which results in all four dogs ending up in each of the four cars, preparatory to the next phase of the story, which continues in the following fashion:

'Now this little boy, named Tommy, came along. He went up and started talking to one of the dogs.' (Recall that the boy doll was moved around by me, not the child.) See them talking? Well, they talked and talked, and now, while they were talking, suddenly {a, the} dog drove away. Suddenly {same article} dog drove away.' (This repetition was used occasionally.) This story ends with the boy being put into the boat and all of the characters having a ride down the wooden hill.

Story 3. *Lion and Rabbits.* In this story the toys included a plastic lion, a plastic tiger, four wooden rabbits, and a few green plastic bushes for atmosphere. I moved the lion and tiger, while the child had command of the rabbits. As the story begins, the lion and tiger, who move about spasmodically on a plastic base, have just had a fight but have become friends once more:

'The lion and tiger saw the bunnies, and they walked up to them. One of the bunnies went over to the tiger. He said hello to the tiger. Now {a, the} bunny went over to the lion. He said hello to him.' After this there are more interesting events which include the rabbits' getting on the backs of the lion and tiger.

The general strategy for correct answering in all the stories is similar, of course. A definite expression like *the dog* or *the bunny* should be taken as referring to the last conspicuous member of the class nominated. An indefinite reference such as *a dog* or *a bunny* should be understood, at least a good deal of the time, as referring to some other, not yet conspicuous member of the class.

Comments on the construction of the comprehension tasks

Unnaturalness of the wording

One of the most noticeable aspects of the stories, and intentionally so, is the frequent unnaturalness of the definite and indefinite expressions in the story. In most cases the plain indefinite article is quite weak as a reference shifting device. To insure a shift of reference with the other animals or objects present, a speaker would more normally have used an expression like *another dog* or *one of the other dogs*. Where the definite expressions were used, *the same X* would have served better, though the disparity does not seem as great. It follows from the mildly unnatural character of the sentences that when children respond properly to the distinct forms, they must be understanding them on the basis of some sort of rule-guided system of interpretation.

Other aspects of the wording

The crucial definite and indefinite expressions were always the subjects of their sentences. The phonological distinction between *a* and *the* is already a fine one, easily missed. To have put test cases in object position (and so in the middle of the sentences) might have detracted from the child's hearing the distinction at all. The use of *now* and *suddenly* to precede the articles has already been commented on.

In all cases the expression *one of the Xs* (e.g. 'One of the dogs jumped on the table') was always used to introduce the first member of a class. In this way, the indefinite article *a* was never employed to introduce a referent prior to the test expression. Such a precaution was taken in order to insure that the children would not discover the procedure of introducing single referents with simple indefinites from the wording of the stories, though it always seemed implausible that this might occur.

Sex of toy children

As described in each story, whenever a toy child was used, it was always a male. When listening to a tape during pilot investigations, I noticed that expressions like *a chair* could easily be taken to sound like a poorly pronounced version of *her chair*, a confusion which would lead to both correct and incorrect false responses. With male actors the analogous confusion is extremely unlikely (*a chair* confused as *his chair*).

Length of the tests

As should be clear from a description of the stories, the tests for comprehension were embedded in rather long-winded stories. There was always more playing than was necessary for the actual tests. What was the purpose of such length?

The major reason was that I wished the crucial tests to be as little test-like as possible. The best way of doing this, and one natural in the case of context-bound morphemes like articles, was to make the crucial answers part of a wider play activity, such as telling or acting out a story, or playing a game. In the case of the comprehension tasks in particular, it was possible to embed the crucial actions by the child in a large series of otherwise similar play activities by making the stories longer.

Another major reason was to make the sessions more enjoyable as a whole. Children enjoyed the comprehension tests greatly, more than any of the other tests. All three stories could probably have been given consecutively with no boredom on the children's parts. The comprehension tasks often aroused or revived the children's general interest, and they proved to be a relaxing interlude from some of the more demanding of the tests, especially for the three-year-olds. Children of both age groups would sometimes ask to do the stories over again. Letting the stories go on a bit longer made matters more enjoyable for all the subjects, and in the end I think increased the quality of their responses.

Distribution of the tests

As summarized earlier, three comprehension testing periods, one corresponding to each story, were distributed among the two experimental sessions. Each child received all three stories, and received two definite article and two indefinite article tests. In story 1 the two test articles always consisted of one definite and one indefinite. Each age group had twenty children, and a distribution was made up for twenty children that was repeated for each age group. Within this distribution each test of any article appeared equally often in each of the comprehension periods. Each child received either *he* or *one* in the pronominal reference tests, but not both. Appendix I lists further details of the distribution.

The results of testing

The results can be initially stated quite briefly. Children in all age and sex groups displayed well above chance comprehension of the distinction between the articles. The entire group of 40 children had an average accuracy of 0.85, with 95 per cent confidence intervals of ± 0.06. The overall accuracy was reliably greater than chance, $t(39) = 12.06$, $p < 0.0001$ (unless otherwise noted, all significance values are for two-tailed tests). I have listed the accuracies of each of the four sex and age groups of the study in table 4.1. There is clearly no effect of either sex or age, and an analysis of variance indicates that the strongest effect obtained is one for sex, $F(1.36) = 1.06$, $p > 0.25$.

There were, however, differences in accuracy of responses to the definite and indefinite expressions. Children chose a referent for *the X* accurately 0.94 of the time, while they chose a new referent for *a X* expressions 0.76 of the time, a reliable difference $F(1.39) = 9.95$, $p < 0.001$.

These results do not include the outcomes of the pronominal tests (*he* vs *one*). The results for these tests are listed in table 4.2. Again competence appears well established for each age group. The three-year-olds' accuracy reliably exceeds chance level performance, $x^2 = 5.00$, $p < 0.05$ as does the accuracy of the four-year olds ($x^2 = 16.20$, $p < 0.001$). The four-year-olds distinguish a little more sharply between the two pronouns, but this difference is not a reliable one ($x^2 = 2.50$, $p > 0.10$).

Discussion of the results

Children apparently comprehend delicate differences in the meaning of definite and indefinite expressions very soon after they have begun stable spontaneous production. Both age groups showed high accuracy

Table 4.1. *Comprehension tests: accuracies for all groups (a X and the X only)*

	3-year-olds	4-year-olds
Males	0.825	0.825
Females	0.900	0.850

Table 4.2. *Responses for pronoun comprehension test*

	Three-year-olds	
	Same referent moved	Different referent moved
He	8	2
One	2	8
	$x^2 = 5.00, p < 0.05$	
	Four-year-olds:	
	Same referent moved	Different referent moved
He	10	0
One	0	10
	$x^2 = 16.20, p < 0.001$	

of comprehension, with no change evident over time. To distinguish in comprehension between the two kinds of expressions as well as they did, the children must have constructed a well generalized system related to the prominence or lack of prominence of a referent in a discourse context to the definiteness of the expressions which refer to it.

The major difference of any kind that was obtained was that errors were more common in response to indefinite articles than to definite articles. Children failed to shift referents 0.24 of the time when hearing *a X*, while the error rate in response to definite expressions was just 0.06. How can this result be explained?

I believe there are two principal alternative explanations, one of them methodological and the other more basic. The methodological one is straightforward. The comprehension stories were constructed and told so as to make certain that the children clearly attended to the prominent member of the class. When confused or uncertain, or not hearing the relevant sound clearly, a child may have tended, as natural response, to choose the most conspicuous member of the set in continuing the story. More errors in response to the indefinite articles would have resulted quite directly from such a response bias. With the tests of pronouns, the distinctive words were the clearly distinguishable *he* and *one*, and here no difference in accuracy obtained between the definite and indefinite form.

On the other hand, if the greater error rate for indefinites resulted from non-comprehending performance, we might expect that errors in responses to indefinites would have decreased in the older group, as did errors in response to pronouns. In fact, accuracy in interpreting indefinite article expressions was 0.78 for the three-year-olds and 0.75 for the four-year-olds. The greater error rate found in the case of indefinites may stem instead from an actual aspect of the semantic understanding of articles. Two major ways of comprehending indefinite article expressions were proposed earlier in the discussion. One of these ways is to interpret an expression of the form *a X* as automatically referring to a new member of the set. The second way was to interpret *a X* as referring to 'any member' of the class. If children did interpret the indefinite article in this fashion, they would feel free to choose any referent to continue the story. In all of the comprehension tests, in fact, there were four of the relevant class available in each situation, whether dogs, chairs, or rabbits. Children feeling free to choose any member of the set randomly would pick the already prominent one just 0.25 of the time by chance, a correspondence to the obtained error rate of 0.24 that is almost too neat. Interestingly, I have occasionally given these tests to adults, and they often argue that, say, *a dog* just means any of the dogs, which could include the dog already prominent in the story. Such conscious intuitions are not to be trusted. But it is a fact that the responses of the two groups of children were quite alike, a finding we shall not generally obtain elsewhere. I believe, then, that the results do support the children's operating with a very general principle of interpretation that expressions of the form *a X* refer to 'any member' of the set very early, and using such an interpretation stably for some period afterwards.

Comprehension versus production

Our initial assessment of children's understanding the semantics of definite and indefinite articles shows a well-generalized formulation of the basic distinction between specificity and non-specificity. At least the competence is reliable and generalized enough to extend comfortably to somewhat unnaturally worded comprehension situations. Since the semantics of definite and indefinite mirror each other considerably in production and comprehension, comprehension at a skilled level implies a considerable corresponding productive competence. Nevertheless these comprehension tasks leave many other aspects of comprehensive and productive competence unassessed. All reference is to concrete, present members of the relevant set. There is no test here for discourse about absent referents or about hypothetical situations. Understanding of the 'no particular member' sense of indefinites found in 'Margaret doesn't have *a car*' can scarcely be assessed by such concrete situations as well. Furthermore, the tests are not completely unambiguous in what competence they show. The child may be operating with more limited kinds of linguistic routines, though still undoubtedly ones of some generalizability and abstraction.

Furthermore, at best the comprehension tests only probe the child's understanding of an aspect of the specific-non-specific dimension of reference. Little in these tests assesses the child's knowledge of the non-egocentric reference implicit in the correct usage of definite and indefinite expressions. As the comprehension stories were told, referents were made clearly prominent or not in the story contexts for both the child and myself. What would be needed to test the child's (and the adult's) non-egocentric comprehension abilities would be a situation where the child's attention is somehow made to focus on a referent other than the one prominent for the speaker. Such situations did occasionally occur by chance in these comprehension tasks. After I had made a particular dog, say, prominent in the *dogs and cars* story, a child might put his hand on another of the dogs, apparently preparing to move that dog into play. It seems reasonable to say that the child was then personally focused on a dog other than the one made prominent in the context by the story. At such times, when I said *the dog* did something, non-egocentric comprehension would consist of moving the dog made prominent by my actions and not the child's own intentions. I did notice a very small number of such incidents, about six. In five, in fact, the child picked the referent prominent for both of us, and not the one he was attending to. If this kind of situation could be produced experimentally in a more regular way, it would constitute a quite stringent test of the subject's non-egocentric comprehension. I believe, though, that most experimental paradigms that met this requirement would necessarily involve considerable artificiality and difficulties of interpretation, though this may only be a limitation on my own ingenuity.

In summary, the results discussed in this chapter show a good understanding of much of the specific–non-specific referential character of articles. But for tests of more abstract and non-egocentric abilities, we must turn to another kind of procedure. In the next chapters I shall discuss work with such procedures and the results which followed.

5
Stories: a description of the tests

Problems for assessment

The central concern in these studies was the *abstractness* of the child's referential abilities: how well caŋ young children use definite and indefinite articles when speaking of fictional stituations, without the support of toys, pictures, or even a memory of real events? In the succeeding sections I shall outline the particular problems that were studied, and the method of study as well.

Definite reference

Definite by previous mention
One convenient way of introducing a discourse referent into a conversation is by mention. Consider a story that was told to children in pilot work for this study. There is initially a man who has been walking through a jungle. The man sees a monkey and a pig. They are having a race. By virtue of the man's having seen *a monkey* and *a pig*, there is now a member of each class that has been introduced to the child. Succeeding references to either ought to be made with definite expressions, i.e. *the monkey* or *the pig*. Children were asked to make just such references. After being told that a monkey and pig were having a race, the child was asked 'Who won the race?' to which the answer should be *the monkey* or *the pig*.

This procedure was typical of the procedure for any of the stories. I told an initial part of the story, which I shall refer to generally from now on as the *preparation*. The preparation led up to a choice point in which some character did something, or some object was chosen, and the child was to indicate his choice. Of course, the preparations were designed so that either a definite or indefinite expression would be appropriate, at least according to adult intuitions. The child's part of the story, in which he makes the choice, will be referred to as the *answer*.

It will be convenient as well to have a brief means of referring to the kind of linguistic test embodied by each story. In the monkey–pig story, for example, the crucial aspect of the preparation is that a particular monkey and pig are introduced, by the means of saying *a monkey* and *a pig*. The answer should consist of a definite expression, *the monkey* or *the pig*. I shall symbolize this kind of preparation–answer relation in the stories by the following means: $aX \to$ the X. The expression to the left of the arrow refers to the crucial reference in the preparation, while the expression on the right refers to the correct answer.

Definite by entailment: $\emptyset \to$ the X

The monkey–pig story provides an example in which a discourse referent is introduced by overt mention, an important category, of definite reference in conversations. But as the discussion of chapter 1 makes clear, there is no mechanical rule of discourse that after a phrase of the form *a X*, future conversational references to X should be of the form *the X*. Some expressions *a X* do not introduce any referent at all. Such cases include cases of negation like 'I never had *a dog*' or some cases of reference to any member, such as 'I am looking for *a dog*, but can't find one.' We shall shortly inspect such cases more closely.

Another means of introducing definite references was also discussed in chapter 1, that of entailment. The conversational context provides a particular X as a discourse referent even though X is not mentioned overtly. The examples discussed in chapter 1 tended to be of the whole–part variety. For example, once one has mentioned someone driving a car, it is possible to speak of *the motor* dying, or *the hood* flying up without an overt introductory mention of either part. A motor and a hood form a part of a car, so mentioning the latter entails the existence of the former. Another means of entailment, investigated briefly in our studies, is part–whole entailment, in which the parts entail a whole. Suppose one states there were two animals. One of them was barking and the other meowing. One could now ask, 'One of them ran away. Who ran away?' to which the answer ought to be *the dog* or *the cat*. Such a paradigm may be symbolized

$$\emptyset \to the\ X$$

in which ∅ symbolizes the absence of any overt reference to X in the preparation. Entailment, then, comprises a second major way of introducing a discourse referent into a conversation, one that was investigated, though only briefly, in these studies.

Indefinite reference

Indefinite by lack of unique specification: Xs → a X
Appropriate definite reference to a member of X rests on the fulfillment of a number of requirements on the referential status of *X*. Essentially, there must be an existent member of X to refer to, and that member must be an already uniquely specified member of X, for speaker and listener alike. We may make an indefinite reference appropriate by removing various of these referential factors, deleting one or more at a time. How may just prior uniqueness, for example, be removed? Consider the following story, again one told to children in pilot investigations. The child was told of a boy and his father who went to a pet store to buy a pet for the boy. They saw many dogs and cats at the store and bought one of them. The child was asked 'What did they take home?'

The proper answer, clearly, is an indefinite, either *a dog* or *a cat*. The preparation established the existence of a number of dogs and cats, among them whatever animal the child chose for his answer. Both the possible class identity (dog or cat) and the existence of the referent have been established before the child's answer. But whatever the child chooses, perhaps a dog, that dog lacks prior specified uniqueness among the dogs mentioned. No particular dog or cat had been introduced in the story before the one the child himself introduces in the answer. Should the child imagine for himself a particular dog being selected and picked up to be taken home, that dog is established as a unique referent only for himself, not his listener. To refer to the animal as *the dog* would hence be an egocentric response, for the listener cannot retrieve a unique specification for the chosen dog. This paradigm, in which just prior uniqueness of the referent is lacking, may be symbolized *Xs → a X*.

Removing existence: a X → a X.
As we have seen previously, it is quite possible to say *a X* without establishing the existence of any referent at all, in sentences like

'I can't drive *a car*', or 'John was trying to find *a tiger* but couldn't find one.' Such indefinites introduce no referents, and succeeding references to the class nominated by *X* often should be indefinite ones. The appropriate symbolization for such a paradigm is then $a\,X \to a\,X$. This paradigm may be further divided into at least two different potential referential paradigms. I shall briefly preview two of the stories to explicate this. In one of the stories, children were told about a man who went to a jungle because he wanted to find *a lion* or *a zebra*. After the man wandered around for a while looking for *a lion* or *a zebra*, the child was suddenly asked 'And then who do you think came running out at the man?' Should a lion or zebra be chosen, the answer should clearly be an indefinite. The preparation for the answer introduces no particular lion or zebra at all, and includes not even the existence of a relevant lion or zebra. A particular member of one of the classes is introduced into the discourse only by the child's answer.

We may also ask that the child give an answer by presumably referring to no particular class member at all. In the relevant story the child was told of a boy or girl who was sad by reason of not having *a dog* or *a cat*. The child was then asked 'Which does he like more?' If an article is to be used at all, it should be an indefinite one, as in 'He likes *a dog* more'. Again the child must recognize that the preparation establishes no cat or dog at all to talk about, though establishing classes to talk about, *dog* and *cat*. Furthermore, his own answer should establish no referent either. The answer to such a question is purely generic. It is not that the character of the story likes a particular dog or cat more, but that he likes any dog or cat more. Where convenient, I shall symbolize the last described paradigm as $a\,X \to a\,X$ generic. It is the only story in which the indefinite answer also makes no reference to particular class members.

Removal of class specification: $\emptyset \to a\,X$

Finally, we may introduce an object into a story, in a context that insures its uniqueness – but give it no class specification. In one relevant story, the child was told that the characters of a story suddenly saw an animal that came running out at them. The child was asked 'Who came running out?' (I shall comment later on the slightly unnatural use of *who*.) The child could say *the animal*. But if he wishes to give a more specific reference, perhaps to *tiger*, his answer should be *a tiger*. Definite and indefinite reference are determined by a combination of the existential state of a referent with the knowledge of its class membership. Only previous knowledge of a referent as a unique member of the nominated class makes definite reference allowable, and it is just this class specification that is lacking in the preparation to $\emptyset \to a\ X$ stories.

Summary

The problems discussed above constitute a wide sampling of referential competence. We shall see shortly that even in children's initial use, command of a wide part of the semantic system is present, particularly in the use of the specific–non-specific dimension of the semantics of articles. Before discussing results from the experimental investigations, though, it is necessary to have a fuller description of the stories actually used for this assessment, and of the methodological concerns that entered into their design.

Description of the stories

Preliminary methodological comments

The choice between classes

One awkward aspect of the stories is that the child must always make a choice between two specified classes (except in the paradigm discussed last, $\emptyset \to a\ X$). This constructional artifice was necessary, however, to insure the use of full article + noun answers. Unless specification of the class of a referent is necessary, it is more convenient and natural to use a pronominal reference. Suppose someone said 'I saw a funny looking dog today.' He might well continue reference to the dog by saying *he* or *it* rather than using the full noun phrase *the dog*. On the other hand, if the initial sentence is 'I saw a funny looking dog and a cat today,' a continued reference to the dog must include mention of his class: '*the dog* followed me home'. Saying *it* or *he* would leave unclear whether the dog or cat was intended: 'I saw a dog and a cat today: *he* followed me home.' The story tests thus always required of the child an implicit choice between the two classes in order to insure use of the articles. It was assumed that children would in fact use the fuller phrases with articles as reference, an assumption that proved to be correct.

Contrastive story versions

In initial pilot work, a given story was employed to test competence in just one paradigm, much as in the descriptions above. For example, consider the monkey–pig race story. This story was used to assess children's competence in the *a X → the X* paradigm. Even three-year-olds gave definite expressions as answers with well above chance frequency. Such a pattern of response implies knowledge of the necessary semantic knowledge, but does it really? Suppose children had been given a story about a race between any number of monkeys and pigs, with still one winner, and the same question, 'Who won the race?' They might still have given many definite expressions as answers. Certain situations and stories may tend to elicit preferentially indefinite or definite answers despite delicate contextual changes that should require a change in response.

In the second phase of pilot work, evidence arose that clearly supported this hypothesis. I constructed another *aX → the X* story, one about a man wanting to go somewhere who had a car and a boat. The children were told he used one of them, and asked 'What did he use?' Unlike the monkey–pig race story, this story received a large number of indefinite expressions as answers, particularly from three-year-old children. In fact, I found on making inquiries that even adults occasionally gave an indefinite noun phrase as an answer. I changed the question slightly, substituting *which one* for *what* ('Which one did he use?') and answers became gratifyingly definite in form. In short, it became clear that a given story might have the definiteness of its answer determined at least partly by factors other than the ones supposedly being varied.

In a later discussion of the results we shall find that there is systematic evidence for these propositions: different stories seem to have different base-lines of definiteness associated with them, and even the question word that is used may have systematic effects on the definiteness of the answers. The solution, at least for the testing of many of the paradigms, was a traditional psychological one. Stories were constructed which could be told in two versions, such that either a definite or indefinite expression was the proper answer. Each child was then given either the definite-eliciting or indefinite one of the two eliciting versions for a given story. In this way, only the systematic semantic variables of interest formed the differences between the story versions. Competence could be gauged by the degree of contrastive response to definite- and indefinite-eliciting story versions.

Reducing differences between contrastive story versions entailed using the same question phrase, whether *which one, who, what,* or *which* for both versions of such stories. This inevitably led to occasional unnaturalness. The question words of English are not neutral in their implications for what sort of answer the questioner expects. *Which one* implies that a very specific answer is expected. It would not do, for example, to say someone chose a pet from a group of cats and dogs, and then ask 'Which one did he choose?' Other question phrases are not quite as pointed in their implication, but still have preferred directions. *Who* and *which* are more appropriate for an expected definite answer, while *what* tends to the indefinite though quite appropriate in a number of situations where a definite expression may be expected.

But of course it is not possible to choose the most appropriate question word for a given story version, e.g. *which one* for *a X → the X* and *what* for *Xs → a X.* For then some appropriate contrastive response to the stories might result simply from the child's having learned something about question answering, in particular something about the definiteness of the answer as implied by the form of the question. Clearly the question phrase must be kept identical for both versions of a story, even when the result is somewhat unnatural.

Description of the individual stories

Thirteen stories were devised in all, of which twelve will be described here.[1] Just eight were told in systematically contrastive definite and indefinite-eliciting versions. Each of these stories had a version to which the answer should have been a definite expression and a version requiring an indefinite expression as answer, as regulated by the abstract semantic rules I have been describing. I shall refer to these eight stories as the *systematic stories.* Another four stories were made up for miscellaneous reasons — interest in the form of the question word, testing for entailment, age differences in particular problems; they will accordingly be called the *miscellaneous stories.*

1. A description of the thirteenth story, Hammer–Saw, is to be found in appendix III.

The systematic stories

Each systematic story existed in two versions. One of these versions had a definite expression as proper answer, what I shall call a D version, and the other had an indefinite expression as proper answer (I version). Five of the eight stories were concerned with the following contrast:

I version	D version
$Xs \rightarrow aX$	$aX \rightarrow the\ X$

What follows is a description of each of these five stories, in their differing versions.

1. Making Noise.
   I version: $Xs \rightarrow aX$
   D version: $aX \rightarrow the\ X$

   Once there was a lady. She had (I version: lots of boys and girls, about four girls and three boys; D version: a boy and a girl.) They were very noisy, and they kept her awake all the time. One night she went to bed. She told them to be very quiet. She said, 'If anyone makes any noise, they won't get any breakfast tomorrow.' Then she went to bed. But do you know what happened? One of them started laughing and giggling. (If the I version was being told, E said something like 'Now let's see, there were four girls and three boys.' Children apparently reduce plurals to singular fairly frequently, and so often definite numbers were assigned and reiterated to plural groups to help with this problem.) Who was laughing and giggling like that?

The above description may give some idea of how the stories were told. The child was told he would hear part of a story, and that he was to finish it. A number of the children had to be assured that there was no right answer. They were not worried about getting the articles right, of course. They were worried that either a boy or girl, for example, must have done it, and they would not know. As a result, I could not read off of a sheet or out of a book when telling the stories. When this was attempted once or twice, it became almost impossible to convince some children that there really was not a right answer, down on the sheet with the rest of the story. So on putting away the toys from a previous procedure I looked to see what stories the child was to receive in the particular story period, and told the stories from memory. There were thus small variations in telling the stories, but probably none that affected the outcomes significantly.

2. Out to Meet.

I version: $Xs \rightarrow a\ X$

D version: $a\ X \rightarrow the\ X$

(Usually told in a context of a man or child in a jungle, depending on the preceding story told.) Now the man was very lonely. He saw (I version: some animals; D version: two animals.) He saw (I version: some monkeys and some pigs; D version: a monkey and a pig.) 'Maybe one of those animals will come out and be my friend', he said. And one of them did. Who went out to the man?

3. Pond.

I version: $X\ s \rightarrow a\ X$

D version: $a\ X \rightarrow the\ X$

Roughly, someone with a wooden box goes to a pond to get an animal. He sees (I version: two bunches of animals (frogs and turtles, for example); D version: two animals (a frog and a turtle).) So he puts one of them into his box. What did he put in?

4. Knock Over.

I version: $X\ s \rightarrow a\ X$

D version: $a\ X \rightarrow the\ X$

This story was told previously. An animal, established by either the Pond story or by the story called Like (p. 53), belonged to someone. The animal was described as liking to walk all over chairs and tables. One day it got up on a table that had (I version: lots of glasses and cups; D version: a glass and a cup) on it. Then, the animal knocked over one of them. (I version: a reminder was given of previously assigned numbers of cups and glasses.) What did he knock over?

5. Give.

I version: $X\ s \rightarrow a\ X$

D version: $ax \rightarrow the\ X$

Pretend you have (I version: lots of turtles and lots of squirrels, say four turtles and four squirrels; D version: two animals, a turtle and a squirrel.) Now pretend your mommy wanted one of your animals. Would you give her one? (If the child said no, he was told that sure he would.) Well, what would you give her?

The last story, Give, provides an example of a case where the two conditions may not absolutely determine different responses. A few adults have told me that they thought an indefinite expression might be appropriate as an answer for the D version of the story. They answered, in effect, 'I would give her a turtle in such a case', ignoring the particular hypothetical turtle mentioned in the story. It is probably the hypothetical nature of the story that results in this slight optionality. Still, the D version far more clearly takes definite expressions as a proper answer than does the I version.

The other three systematic stories assessed competence in handling stories which contrasted the following contrast:

I version	D version
$a\ X \to a\ X$	$a\ X \to the\ X$

One of the stories provided an instance where the answer should properly refer to no animal at all, i.e. $a\ X \to a\ X$ generic:

6. Like.
   I version: $a\ X \to a\ X$ generic
   D version: $a\ X \to the\ X$
   I know a little boy (or girl) and he is very (I version: sad; D version: happy.) Do you know why? Well, (I version: he doesn't have a dog or a cat; D version: he's got a dog and a cat.) (E repeats last statement.) Which does he like more?

   In the case where the boy has a dog and a cat, 'Which does he like more?' means which of them — the cat or the dog? In the case where the boy doesn't have a dog or a cat, the question, 'Which does he like more?' can only mean 'What kind of animal does he like more?' since there is no dog or cat to talk about. This latter case was discussed earlier on p. 47. The use of *which* as a question word is the same for both versions, as always; this does not affect the validity of the test.

In the other two stories in which the I version was $a\ X \to a\ X$, the indefinite answer actually does refer to an existent X:

7. Looking For.
   I version: $a\ X \to a\ X$.
   D version: $a\ X \to the\ X$.
   In this story, discussed earlier (p. 47), a man went to a jungle or forest, because he wanted to see a lion or a zebra (for example). So he went off looking for a lion or a zebra. (Indefinites were used repetitively: 'He looked all over, to see if he could find a lion or a zebra. He looked for a lion or a zebra everywhere.' If properly understood, this makes clear that the man was looking for no particular lion or zebra.) He looked and looked. (I version: story goes directly to final question; D version: then the man found a lion and a zebra together.) Who came running out at the man?

8. Toy.

   I version: $a X \rightarrow a X$.

   D version: $a X \rightarrow the\ X$

   The story is about a boy (or girl) who is having a birthday. In the I version, the boy tells his father, at home, that he wants a tractor and a truck. His father says he can have just one. The boy says he wants both. This goes on for a while. Finally the boy concedes. The father goes off to the toy store, and the subject was asked, 'What did he buy?' In the D version, the father and the boy are at a toy store, and the argument takes place after the boy shows the father a particular tractor and truck and says he wants both. The point was to try to contrast the situation where a toy is actually present to refer to vs that where the categories are mentioned, but no particular members.

These eight systematic stories comprised the major tests of distinctive responding to D and I paradigms, as constructed according to the semantic principles of definite and indefinite reference.

Miscellaneous stories

The four miscellaneous stories each properly fall into a single semantic paradigm. Each story was designed to gain information about children's understanding of a specific semantic problem, without necessarily contrasting systematically with another version of the same story.

The first of these stories, Car—Boat, has been outlined previously. This story was told in two different versions; in one the question word was the definite-eliciting phrase *which one*, and in the other, the more indefinite *what*:

   1. Car—Boat.

      $a X \rightarrow the\ X$

      A man was going to a jungle. Children were told that he had a car and a boat, and used one of them to go to the jungle. In the definite question-form version the child was asked, '*Which one* did he use?' In the indefinite version he was asked, '*What* did he use."

   2. Barking.

      $\emptyset \rightarrow the\ X$

      This story was intended to test for the production of noun phrases made definite by entailment. The type of entailment used here is part—whole entailment, or situation entailment. This story, discussed earlier, told that two animals were playing together, and one of them was barking and the other meowing; a listener can deduce that a particular cat and dog were playing together, and

talk about *the cat* or *the dog*. The child was then told that one of the
animals ran away, and asked 'Who ran away?' The answer should
be definite. Most of the examples discussed earlier of entailment
and those examples which Brown found were examples of wholes
entailing parts: e.g. a car entails a particular horn belonging to it.
In this story, the part (the sound made by the animal) entails the
whole (the kind of animal).

3. No Name.

$\emptyset \rightarrow a X$

This story-type was intended to contrast with the $\emptyset \rightarrow the X$
(entailment) story in particular. In the middle of a story sequence,
the child was told that some animal came running out at the
characters already present, and asked, 'Who came running out at
them?' Or he might have been told that the characters saw
something, and asked, 'What did they see?' Note the slightly
anomalous use of *who* in the subject-position question. This was
done to keep the question word *who* in all questions about
grammatical subjects. There is one important way in which this
story-type fails to match the $\emptyset \rightarrow the X$ story, however: it does not
involve a choice between two possibilities.

4. Cave.

$Xs \rightarrow a X$

The child was told that there were some children, lots of boys and
lots of girls, four of each, who were out playing. Suddenly it began
to rain. The children went into a cave to get out of the rain. They
built a fire inside to stay warm. Finally they wanted to go outside
and see if it was still raining. So they sent someone outside. The
child was reminded that there were four boys and four girls, and
then asked, 'So who do you think went outside?' The interest of
this story lay in the fact that in pilot investigations, a large number
of children gave definite expressions as response. The story was
therefore told in the indefinite-eliciting form to each child in the
study, to investigate possible differences between the three- and
four-year-olds. It was also given to ten randomly chosen parents of
children in the study, to see if systematic differences existed
between the parents and their children.

Final methodological comments

Advantages and disadvantages

The virtues of stories as assessment devices are clear ones. They provide
an apportunity to test the child's competence in making reference to
non-present, fictional referents, or indeed to no referents at all. Earlier

I described a dimension of concreteness of references, from reference to present concrete objects to a very abstract end, and it is on the abstract end that the child must function to answer the questions put to him. Simultaneously, because it is possible to control firmly the contexts and situations the child must respond to, we can assess the child's control of subtle referential distinctions in a way not feasible with observational data.

Yet it should be emphasized that the stories as an assessment technique provide many difficulties not strictly germane to their purposes. They are often long and difficult to keep track of; the child is asked to remember varying numbers of referents in complex situations, and asked to comprehend and store subtle nuances of what has been recounted to him. Finally, the child's production of articles is elicited by a question rather than following in a strictly spontaneous fashion, a procedure that may provide its own difficulties. Later we shall discuss procedures and results that indicate possible effects of these memory and procedural problems, particularly with the three-year-old subjects. The stories, by design, also involve serious differences from more normal conditions of use in other ways. In particular, the child has not had personal experience with the referents spoken about. He must, effectively, construct them on the spot. Again we shall find reason to believe that problems of interpretation may result from these difficulties, problems that require detailed analysis of the data for resolution.

More naturalistic procedures
It is natural to consider at this point whether it might not have been possible to engage the child's knowledge by means of more normal conversational situations. One major problem with this solution, of course, is that we thereby lose a great deal of precise control of the referential situations the child speaks about. It is doubtful that more spontaneous speech could have been elicited in a number of these paradigms. An accompanying difficulty is that the young child, particularly the young three-year-old, is no great *raconteur*. Many mothers attempted to persuade their children to talk about past events to me when I visited at home. Their efforts were largely failures. Even pilot attempts at employing slightly less artificial probing methods, such as asking the child 'What happened next?' at selected points in the stories, failed utterly. The answer was too often a straightforward 'I don't know' that resisted any amount of urging. There is no question

but that these stories are a little artificial and even pushy. But these may have been necessary aspects of their design.

Distribution of the tests

The stories were spread over four periods of testing throughout the two experimental sessions. As was the case for the comprehension tests, the different stories and their versions were spread as evenly as possible over the periods of testing. Simultaneously, the different types of tests — definite-eliciting and indefinite-eliciting — were distributed as evenly as possible within each child (see appendix iii for a complete description).

One aspect of the design deserves note here, however. It became obvious that the three-year-olds especially often did not enjoy telling those stories that were unaccompanied by toys of any kind. Consequently it seemed like a good idea to delete any stories that might cause special difficulty. By chance the first group of children seen experimentally were largely four-year-olds, and even these more advanced subjects had some difficulties with two of the thirteen stories, Toy and Hammer—Saw (see appendix iii for a description of this last story). In Toy, for example, a boy argues with his father because he wants both a truck and a tractor. When asked what toy was finally bought, these four-year-olds sometimes initially said 'both' or responded even more confusedly. A little pilot work with a few three-year-olds confirmed that the Toy and Hammer—Saw stories caused even more confusion to the younger subjects. Consequently I told neither of these two stories to the three-year-old children. Aside from this, the same design was replicated for both age groups.

6
Results from the systematic stories; imitations with expansions

A preliminary analysis

In this chapter I shall discuss largely the results from the systematic stories. The outcomes of the various miscellaneous tests, with the exception of one, the Cave story, will be discussed in a subsequent chapter. At the end of this chapter, however, it will turn out to be fitting to discuss as well the results from the procedure called *imitations with expansions* for the light they shed on the story results. As we shall see, the results discussed in this chapter are the most complex that we shall have to consider. Before the analyses are completed, the simple division into two developmental groups, three-year-olds and four-year-olds will have proven to be too gross; and an analysis of story results according to their paradigmatic type will also be required. I begin initially, nevertheless, with a more general analysis of the competence shown by the two age groups in responding to the systematic stories. In these analyses I shall employ results just from the seven systematic stories told to both age groups.

An overall analysis

In order to have an initial basis for analyzing scores, each child in the study was given an overall score for his response to the systematic stories. Each child was first given two scores: one for his accuracy in answering D (definite-eliciting) versions of systematic stories and one for his accuracy in responding to I (indefinite-eliciting) versions. Only full noun phrases of the form Article + Noun were tabulated.[1] A child's overall accuracy score was then computed as the average of the two separate scores for the D and I conditions.

---

1. Very occasionally in these tests and in the playing of games (chapter 8), a child or adult would give the more exact indefinite form *one of the X's* rather than *a X*. Such occurrences were quite uncommon (once in the stories, twice in the games) and were counted as indefinite expressions. One four-year-old child ingeniously answered *the biggest girl* to the Cave story, which is a correct definite expression. This answer was not tabulated.

Thirty-nine of the forty children gave usable responses in both conditions. (One three-year-old boy, otherwise quite competent, hated the stories with an absolute hate, and could only be persuaded to tell the story called Give, in the I version. When this was useful in analyses of variance, he was assigned the mean of the three-year-old boys for the D condition.) The overall accuracy of the thirty-nine children was 0.79, a performance reliably greater than chance performance of 0.50, $t(38) = 11.20, p < 0.001$.

Group differences
An analysis was also conducted to investigate whether differences in accuracy were to be found between age or sex groups, or between D and I versions of the stories. No effects associated with sex were to be found. The four-year-olds did answer with reliably greater accuracy than the three-year-olds, $F(1.36) = 6.35, p < 0.05$. The four-year-olds' accuracy was 0.85, reliably above chance, $t(19) = 13.17, p < 0.001$. The three-year-olds nevertheless answered with an accuracy of 0.73, still well above chance, $t(18) = 5.61, p < 0.001$.

The analysis of variance indicates that the age difference in accuracy, however, depends on the type of story being tested. ($F(1.36) = 16.38$, $p < 0.001$ for the interaction of condition with age.) The three- and four-year-olds responded to I version stories with accuracies of 0.83 and 0.79 respectively, quite similar accuracies. The large difference in accuracy appears in responding to definite-eliciting stories. The three-year-olds responded to these with an accuracy of just 0.61, far lower than the 0.95 accuracy displayed by the four-year-olds; the difference is reliable at the 0.01 level (Scheffe's Test for Unplanned Comparisons). From these results it seems that children establish an early high degree of competence in responding to I versions of these stories; competence improves largely in giving definite expressions as answers where required. In the next pages, however, I shall show that this two-stage representation of developing competence is incorrect. We shall see that the data justify making a division into three developmental groups, with important effects on the developmental picture obtained.

The division into three developmental groups

The Cave Story
The evidence that we shall consider is evidence gathered from sources other than the systematic stories. The crucial beginning point lies in the

results from the Cave story. This story, as described earlier, was a *Xs* → *a X* story, told in that version to all of the children and to ten randomly selected parents. To review briefly, the story concerned a group of boys and girls stuck in a cave because of rain who eventually sent one of themselves outside to see if it was still raining. So one went outside to see. The child was asked 'Who do you think went out?' The point of this story was that perhaps because of its vividness and detail, many children in pilot work gave an incorrect egocentric answer, saying *the boy* or *the girl* went out, even though the listener had not yet had any particular boy or girl introduced to him. The story seemed to succeed in focusing the child's attention on a particular boy or girl for himself, and so answering egocentrically.

As testing actually turned out, fourteen of the thirty-three children who answered the Cave story incorrectly gave definite responses. In comparison, the ten parents all answered correctly. The results support the hypothesis that children would produce more egocentric references than a mature adult group, $p < 0.05$ by exact test. The two age groups seemed to give about equal proportions of erroneous responses. Eight of nineteen answers were definite expressions among the four-year-olds, and six of fourteen among the three-year-olds, a high proportion of errors for indefinite-eliciting stories in each group.

In the case of both age groups, I wondered whether or not incorrect responses here would not correlate to story responses somewhere else, such as the *Xs* → *a X* versions of the systematic stories. In the case of the four-year-olds, as will be discussed shortly, this seemed to be the case. But even more striking evidence for the non-homogeneity of the four-year-olds came when the Cave story results were compared to results of the imitations.

Imitation results added in

As mentioned earlier, each child in the study was given fourteen sentences to imitate. These sentences ranged in difficulty from easy ones like *I am very tall* to rather complex sentences such as *The boy that the man saw started to laugh*. The intent of this procedure was to obtain some measure of linguistic-cognitive maturity besides age. When the four-year-olds were scored by how many perfect imitations each child obtained, a remarkably strong association emerged between a child's imitation score and the correctness of his answer to the Cave story. A simple inspection of the imitation scores of the two four-year-old groups illustrates the degree of the split quite clearly:

Scores of correct answerers:
14, 14, 13, 13, 13, 12, 11, 11, 10, 10, 9
Scores of incorrect answerers:
9, 8, 6, 6, 5, 5, 4, 3.

The split is extremely reliable, $t(17) = 8.11$, $p < 0.001$. I later scored imitations by a more continuous method which allowed scores between 0 and 1 (cf. appendix v); the resulting split was identical. Apparently scores on imitations could be employed as an independent variable to divide the four-year-olds into two groups, with a division point around nine or ten perfect imitations. Nine vs ten was chosen as the boundary in order to give an extra child to the lower competence group, which was smaller in number. The number of lower group subjects was thus nine, versus eleven in the upper group.

A further analysis of the two four-year-old groups showed that the higher imitators told the systematic stories with an accuracy of 0.93, compared to an accuracy of 0.76 for the lower group; these accuracies differed reliably, $t(18) = 3.04$, $p < 0.01$. There seems to be ample evidence to divide the four-year-olds into two groups, based on their performance on imitations and the Cave story.

No such evidence exists for the three-year-olds. Neither responses on the Cave stories nor overall accuracy corresponded to any reliable trend in imitation scores. Children who answered the Cave story incorrectly had an average continuous imitation score of 8.91 compared to 7.65 for those who answered correctly. This is consistent, for the more mature group of children might be expected to be more like the lower four-year-olds, and so be inaccurate, in answering the Cave story. But the difference between the groups' imitation scores falls far short of statistical significance, $t(12) < 1$, $p > 0.25$. This failure to obtain a competence division probably lay in two major causes. The three-year-olds largely included children in only the six-month range from three to three-and-a-half years of age, with the exception of a two-year, eight-month-old girl. The range of competence should thus be constricted compared to the four-year-olds, whose ages extended throughout a whole twelve-month interval. The three-year-olds also displayed far more variability in how they responded to the imitations. Two of the three-year-old girls would not do them at all. Some who did respond sometimes clearly did not take them seriously. One responded to 'I like to ride in cars' with 'So what' before she could be coaxed to give a more appropriate imitation. The four-year-olds, in contrast, nearly all attempted the imitations with great seriousness. The greater variation of reaction among the three-year-olds should accordingly reduce the discriminative power of the test.

On the basis of the above results, it seems justifiable to split the two age groups into three for further analysis: children three-and-a-half and under, to be called 3 All; the less able four-year-olds, to be called 4 Low; and the abler four-year-olds, the 4 High.

Analysis of the results with three groups

In the discussion that follows, all analyses will be based solely on the results from the seven systematic stories given to both groups (i.e. results from the Toy story will not be used). If we compute overall accuracies as before, the accuracies of the 3 All, 4 Low, and 4 High groups respectively are 0.73, 0.76, and 0.93. The data seem to show a sharp break between the 4 Low and 4 High groups. There were, however, two kinds of contrasts tested by these stories: $a X \rightarrow a X$ vs $a X \rightarrow the X$ and $Xs \rightarrow a X$ vs $a X \rightarrow the X$. The results will be analyzed for each contrast separately.

Analysis of Xs → a X *vs* a X → the X

The difference between the D and I versions of these stories lies in the failure of the $Xs \rightarrow a X$ stories (like the Cave story) to establish a unique member of a class, a discourse referent, before the child's answer. The child is asked to choose one member from a group of referents as his answer. Though whatever referent he chooses has had its existence established in the preparation for the story, the referent lacks specification that gives it previous uniqueness as a class member. In the $a X \rightarrow the X$ preparation, in contrast, there is only one member of each class, so that a unique member of each class is established as discourse referent for both the child and listener, and definite reference becomes appropriate.

The overall accuracies for the 3 All, 4 Low, and 4 High groups in responding to the $Xs \rightarrow a X$ vs $a X \rightarrow the X$ stories were, respectively, 0.69, 0.68, and 0.97. Again we find a break between the 4 High group and the rest. The 4 High group is reliably more accurate than the 4 Low group, $t(17) = 3.77$, $p < 0.002$. The 4 Low and 3 All groups are practically equivalent in accuracy once again.

But even this level of analysis masks important differences among the responses of the three groups. Suppose we analyze the results for the indefinite-eliciting $Xs \to a\,X$ stories and the definite-eliciting $a\,X \to$ *the X* paradigms for each developmental group. The resulting scores are summarized in table 6.1.

Table 6.1. *Accuracies of the 3 All, 4 Low, and 4 High groups in the* Xs → a X *versus* a X → the X *paradigms*

	Paradigm		
Group	$Xs \to a\,X$	$a\,X \to the\,X$	Overall accuracy
3 All	0.83	0.55	0.69
4 Low	0.42	0.94	0.68
4 High	0.98	0.97	0.98

The 4 High group is essentially perfect in response to both paradigms. But now it can be seen that although the overall accuracies of the 3 All and 4 Low groups are almost identical, these accuracies result from quite different patterns of response. Let us look at the pattern of results for each of the 4 Low and 3 All groups separately.

Analysis for the 4 Low group
A comparison with the 4 High group shows that the 4 Low children managed very well to refer definitely where called for, in responding to the $a\,X \to the\,X$ stories. But in completing $Xs \to a\,X$ stories, the 4 Low children gave correct indefinite responses just 0.42 of the time; 58 per cent of their responses were incorrect definite expressions. Our analyses have uncovered a developmental stage where egocentric definite responding is quite common. The children fail to take into account that even if they have established for themselves a particular boy or girl, or monkey or pig that does something, that referent is not yet uniquely specified for their listener, and must be introduced to the listener with an indefinite expression. It is appropriate that it is the 4 Low group's responses in the $Xs \to a\,X$ condition that differentiates them so strongly from the 4 High group. Our division of the four-year-olds into the groups began with an analysis of the Cave story, which is simply another $Xs \to a\,X$ story. All but one of the 4 Low children gave an incorrect definite response to this story, while none of the 4 High group answered incorrectly.

Analysis for the 3 All group

The 3 All group made few egocentric errors in answering the $Xs \rightarrow a X$ stories. Eighty-three per cent of their responses to $Xs \rightarrow a X$ stories consisted of correct indefinite expressions. But this outcome is unlikely to have stemmed from a lack of egocentrism on their parts, given what we know of the presumably more advanced 4 Low group's responses. For a true non-egocentric response, a speaker must have a referent clearly in mind as a particular, unique member of its class before referring to it, yet still introduce it with an indefinite noun phrase. The $Xs \rightarrow a X$ stories are designed to make this precondition a difficult one to fulfill. The preparations of these stories establish just two groups of referents; they mention no particular members of either class. The child is told that one member of the groups did something or was acted on, and is asked to continue. Only if the child can quickly establish and maintain a representation for a unique member of one of the classes immediately upon the request to continue will he be in a position to give an erroneous definite noun phrase response. The 3 All group, in fact, already seems to have had difficulty in establishing and maintaining representations of unique referents well enough to give definite noun phrases consistently as answers to the $a X \rightarrow the X$ stories, in which the preparations clearly set out unique class members: their overall accuracy to responding to the $a X \rightarrow the X$ stories was just 0.61, compared to 0.94 and 0.98 for the two four-year-old groups. It is not surprising, then, that they gave few erroneous definite noun phrase responses to $Xs \rightarrow a X$ stories, in which the task of constructing unique class member representations was made far more difficult. This brief account of the 3 All group's indefiniteness remains quite speculative here and in need of support. Further results to corroborate it will be presented in the discussion to come later of imitations with expansions.

Accuracy in the 3 All and 4 Low groups

After such an emphasis on the difficulties of these groups, it is worth recalling that both the 3 All and 4 Low children showed reliably differential response to the $Xs \rightarrow a X$ vs the $a X \rightarrow the X$ story versions. The 3 All group's accuracy of 0.69 exceeded chance reliably, $t(18) = 4.41$, $p < 0.01$, as did the accuracy (0.68) of the 4 Low group, $t(18) = 2.87$, $p < 0.02$. Despite the abstract nature of the story-telling circumstances, both groups reliably gave more definite expressions when a unique referent had been clearly established, in the *a X → the X* condition, than when one had not, in the *Xs → a X* condition. In short, their linguistic behavior proved to be reliably modulated by the referential circumstances set up by the different story types, and in the appropriate direction. Such performance shows command of the specific—nonspecific dimension and its relevance for use of the articles even in somewhat unnatural circumstances. What is lacking is the finely honed ability both to establish specific reference for onself quickly and simultaneously take into account the point of view of the listener, abilities both present in the members of the 4 High group.

Analysis of a X → a X vs ax → the X

The *Xs → a X* preparations removed one of the conditions for appropriate definite reference: the previous uniqueness among the members of whatever class the child selects. In the *a X → a X* story versions of the systematic stories, as discussed earlier, no unique referent was established at all by the *a X* of the preparation, part of what the child must comprehend. By now the reader may have forgotten the two relevant stories, so I shall review them briefly here.

In Looking For, the child was told that a man was in a jungle, looking for a lion or a zebra. It was repeated that he was trying to find *a zebra* or *a lion* many times. At least to the understanding hearer, this repetition of the indefinite reference establishes that the man was not seeking any particular lion or zebra, or else reference would become definite. In the indefinite-eliciting version, the child was suddenly asked, 'And then who came running out at the man?' The child was not even told first that an animal did come running out, just asked 'Who came running out at the man?' leaving it to him to infer from the insistent repetition of *lion* and *zebra* that one of these is probably the correct answer. In the definite-eliciting version, the man is said to have found a lion and a zebra, establishing referents to talk about; the question was then immediately asked, 'Who came running out at the man?'

In the second story, Like, the child was told that a boy (or girl, depending on the sex of the subject) had a dog and a cat (definite-eliciting version) or did not have a dog or a cat (indefinite-eliciting version). Then he was asked the slightly unnatural question, 'Which does the boy like more?' Again the child must comprehend that the *a X* of the *a X →*

a X preparation establishes no referent to talk about, and the answer should be an indefinite. In the Looking For story, the child's answer presumably actually makes reference to a real lion or tiger. The indefinite answer to the Like story should be about no cat or dog at all.[1]

It may have been the great clarity of the resulting contrast in the definite- and indefinite-eliciting paradigms that results from removing both uniqueness and existence, or it may have been some other feature of the relevant stories; but whatever the cause, competence in answering these apparently abstract stories seems to have begun at a high level and not to have changed markedly. The accuracies of the 3 All, 4 Low, and 4 High groups were 0.82, 0.98, and 0.91 respectively. None of the possible comparisons among the age groups' accuracies even approaches reliability. (For the most extreme comparison, 3 All vs 4 High, $t(28) = 0.94$, $p > 0.25$.) When one considers the inevitable problems the younger group would be expected to have – and did have – because of lesser memories and attention, the lack of any reliable difference between them and the older group is quite convincing.

These results further support a relatively extensive early command by young children of the specific–non-specific referential dimension. It seems clear that their appropriate use of definite references *the X* cannot be traced to a mechanical conversational algorithm of using a definite reference to X after hearing a mention of a phrase *a X*. An inspection of the particular stories shows that correct answering required sensitive inspection of the semantic context to understand the non-referring nature of the indefinite expressions in the *a X → a X* preparations. Children's apparently early established competence in dealing with these referentless indefinite expressions corresponds well to the naturalistic competence found in observation studies.

1. *I was able to continue the conversation about this story with a few of the* four-year-olds, and their conversation gave evidence that they really had no particular dog or cat in mind. But in general one cannot actually tell if a child's answer is a generic indefinite simply from the form of the answer, so this distinction among the indefinite answers is mostly based on adult intuition. In passing, it did sometimes happen that children spontaneously used what were clearly generic indefinites. For example, when dogs were driving cars in one of the comprehension stories, a large number of children, especially four-year-olds, commented 'But *a dog* can't drive a car.'

On the indefiniteness of the three-year-olds: evidence from imitations with expansions

A speculative account of the problem

Though showing a good deal of early competence in extending the specific—non-specific referential factor to the abstract domain of purely fictional reference, the three-year-olds did seem to have some difficulty in making definite references to the story characters. Their references were too often indefinite, as though the referents were not clearly represented or established for them. Such a description, of course, applies only to the group as a whole. Some three-year-olds had little such difficulty. But the group trend was quite clear.

What is the source of this difficulty? In natural discourse these children did not seem overly indefinite, even when occasionally talking about absent referents (though it is true they rarely if ever spoke of purely fictional ones). It seems to me that the difficulties may lie in two sources, one complementing the other: difficulties of memory for context and particular difficulties caused by the means of obtaining responses: asking for choices among two classes.

Difficulties in establishing referential representations

Specific reference follows from the particularity of the referent spoken about, its being a unique member of a specified class. In particular, one must have constructed a mental representation that includes both a specification for class membership and the contextual specifications that make the referent unique among the members of its class. We may imagine that it requires psychological processing time and adeptness to construct such a representation and stabilize it sufficiently for use by the linguistic system. It was an explicit assumption of the discussion that the 4 Low children differed from the 3 All children in being quicker and more adept in constructing and maintaining such representations. Subjectively it was clear in telling the stories that the three-year-olds experienced greater difficulty in following and remembering the stories and their characters. Their difficulties of memory — and sometimes, perhaps resultingly, interest — often made it necessary to go back over stories and repeat parts of them, an extremely rare occurrence with the four-year-old children. When the answer was to be given, the three-year-olds may well have lacked as clear a representation of the referent's unique participation in the story context, leaving them only with a representation of class membership when answering.

Asking for a choice between classes

At the same time, it must be remembered that children were not simply conversing when they gave their answers. The child was questioned to induce production, and requested to make a choice between two possible classes for the referent, between *boy* and *girl*, or *lion* and *zebra*, or *glass* and *cup*, and so on. There was a good deal of implicit emphasis on choosing a class membership for the referent. In general the proper reference for a question about class identity is indefinite. 'What was it?' 'A boy.' Making specific reference requires overcoming and superseding this emphasis on class membership alone, and thinking as well about the contextual uniqueness of the class member. If the child's representational abilities are slightly weak, the emphasis on choice between classes in answer to a question would bias answers to the indefinite pole.

These notions are clearly speculative. But aside from subjective impressions of the younger children's greater difficulty in attending to the stories, I believe they can be supported more substantively. I turn now to a description of the test called imitations and expansions, the design of which I believe may have obviated the cognitive difficulties outlined above. The results that I shall discuss support the above account and also give further support to the claim that children have an early well-developed command of the specific-non-specific semantic dimension even in making relatively abstract reference.

Description of the tests

The essential characteristic of the imitation with expansion tests was that the child imitated, sentence by sentence, a story which I told him. At a crucial point in one sentence, an article was deleted from the model utterance. Children imitating an otherwise grammatical sentence which is missing a small morpheme will often supply the missing morpheme in their imitation (Menyuk, 1963). As the child attains greater control of the construction with maturity, the imitation may be more exact in leaving out the morpheme like the model does. But for some time the tendency to supply it may be strong, and may be employed in testing linguistic competence.

Each child who participated in imitations with expansion received two short stories to imitate. Each story existed in two version, one corresponding to an *Xs* → *a X* paradigm, and the other to an *a X* → *the X* paradigm. I list the two stories, with the appropriate preparations, below:

> Story 1:
> Once there was a man.
> He wanted a pet.
> He went to a petstore.
> *Xs* → *a X*: He saw some *monkeys* there.
> *a X* → *the X*: He saw a *monkey* there.
> So he took ∅ monkey home (test sentence).
>
> Story 2:
> Once there was a boy.
> He wanted to write a letter.
> He went to his mother.
> *Xs* → *a X*: She showed him some *pencils*.
> *a X* → *the X*: She showed him a *pencil*.
> So he took ∅ pencil (test sentence).
> And he wrote his letter.

Children who understand the distinction between the articles should fill in the gap marked by ∅ with *the X* more frequently after an *a X* preparation and more frequently with *a X* after an *Xs* preparation.[1]

The imitations with expansions procedure differs from the earlier story procedures in a number of ways. The answer is not elicited by questioning, and there is no choice to be made among potential classes. The actual stories are quite simple, and the child tells each story him-

---

1. Particular phonological problems did arise with the use of Imitations with Expansions that should be noted. Many three-year-olds did not have the *th* sound in their articulatory repertoires, and used the phoneme /d/ instead, saying 'dat' for 'that', and so on. It was most natural to tell the imitation with expansion stories in the past tense, but many verbs in the past tense end with a /t/ sound. So if one had as an imitative sequence 'He got ∅ banana', the /t/ sound on the end of *got* would make it difficult to know with some children if the child had said 'He got a banana' or 'He got de banana.' In these tests, I used the verb *took* in each sentence, which ends in /k/. After /k/, the distinction between *the* in either correctly or incorrectly pronounced form and *a* is quite clear. In addition, listening to tapes, I found that ∅ after a word such as *saw* usually tended to sound like *a* before the next word, so that 'He saw ∅ monkey' sounds like 'He saw a monkey.' In general, use of the deletion technique required a good bit of pilot work and listening before useful cases could be constructed.

self, repeating each sentence, which should aid in fixing the narrative more firmly in his mind. In this way it was thought possible to see if the indefiniteness characteristic of the three-year olds' performance with Stories was fully general, or could be countered by changes in the experimental task.

Distribution of the tests

Only the three-year-olds received this test. Pilot testing indicated that the four-year-olds were too likely to imitate the articleless sentences exactly, and so leave out the article. In order to insure that the three-year-olds would not have practice in imitating that was not given to the four-year-olds, Imitations and expansions were the very last task administered, coming after the fourteen imitations which served to fix linguistic competence. As usual, each child received each story in just one version, receiving one story in the definite-eliciting version and one in the indefinite-eliciting version.

Results of testing

Eighteen of the twenty three-year-olds agreed to imitate these stories. Twenty-six responses of the form article + noun were obtained, at least one from each child. The other ten responses fell into the following categories: eight times the child did not supply the missing article; one pronoun (*it*) was given and one noun phrase of the form possessive (*his*) + noun was given. I report here on just the twenty-six article + noun responses.

Thirteen of the article + noun responses were given to the $a X \rightarrow the$ X story versions, and thirteen to $Xs \rightarrow a X$ versions. All thirteen of the $a X \rightarrow the X$ responses consisted of definite noun phrases, either *the monkey* or *the pencil*. Responses to the indefinite-eliciting versions consisted of eleven indefinite noun phrases and two definite noun phrases. The indefiniteness characteristic of responses to the systematic stories clearly has disappeared in these answers. Each child was scored for the accuracy of the article + noun response(s) that he gave. The average of these individual scores was then 0.94, an accuracy which reliably exceeded chance, $t(17) = 8.95, p < 0.001$.

Discussion of the results

The two most striking results from this procedure are the greatly increased definiteness of response and the accompanying accuracy of response. As discussed above, the imitations with expansions differed from the stories in a number of possibly important ways: they were briefer and less complicated; production was elicited as part of a whole sentence, continuing a story, rather than as an answer to a question containing a choice between two classes; and the child established the referents and situations of the stories for himself by means of his own speech. Subjectively, it seemed clear that the children's interest in the story-forming imitations was higher than that for the stories. It was not at all uncommon for a child to add something about what might happen next spontaneously, before I could give the next sentence.

On the whole, the greater definiteness of the three-year-olds' responses to these imitations with expansions substantiates the speculations offered earlier about the sources of their indefiniteness, though not determining whether or not one problem or another might have been the more important. The results of the stories may indicate that younger children have some difficulty, comparatively, establishing unique class member representations. But this difficulty, if it exists, does not appear to be a very profound one. The referents of the imitations with expansions task are no less fictional or absent than those of the stories task, yet the only erroneous answers obtained were definite responses.

The other result of interest lies in the great accuracy of response to these tests — accuracy was 0.94, compared with 0.69 for the same contrast tested by the systematic stories ($Xs \rightarrow a\ X$ versus $a\ X \rightarrow the\ X$). One explanation that can be ruled out is that practice over the experimental sessions had increased the children's ability to respond to the tests. A tabulation of accuracies for the four systematic story periods gives average group scores of 0.70, 0.71, 0.73, and 0.65. The subjects did not improve over time in telling stories, so this explanation cannot be seriously entertained.

The greater simplicity of the stories, and the chance for the child to establish the situation for himself have already been mentioned as reasons why incorrect indefiniteness may have vanished. Perhaps the more striking puzzle is why there were not more definite responses (counted here as erroneous) to the $Xs \rightarrow a\ X$ stories. Consider a sequence including a correct response to Story 2:

Model: She showed him some pencils.
Child: She showed him some pencils.

Model: So he took ∅ pencil.
Child: So he took *a* pencil.

At the time the child says 'So he took a pencil', the Model's sentence has already noted a particular pencil. Why were definite expressions as uncommon as they were in this condition?

A number of explanations are available. One explanation, from which these results follow most clearly, is that the child is largely attempting to repeat just what he hears. After the Model and the child say 'She showed him some pencils', the Model's next sentence is 'So he took ∅ pencil.' The child must 'hear' an article, and hear the article he thinks appropriate to hear. My guess is that he believes the Model should have said *a pencil*, because prior to hearing the test sentence, no particular pencil had been made conspicuous to him, the child. The hypothesis presupposes a sophisticated knowledge on the child's part of what he expects to hear from others, given the semantic context, though it does not entail that he knows exactly what he should say to others. Combined with the results obtained in the systematic stories (particularly the results of the *a X → a X* vs *a X → the X* stories), these results then support the notion that the child has quite exact initial knowledge of the principles of specific and non-specific reference even when non-concrete reference is being made.

Summary

A major result of this work, I think, is that we should credit even children just beginning in their use of articles with a considerably generalized knowledge of their use; in particular, they seem to possess extensively generalizable knowledge of the dimension of specificity— non-specificity. Response to contexts in which no referent had been mentioned (*a X → a X*) versus those in which a discourse referent was established (*a X → the X*) was highly discriminating from the beginning in all groups. All groups also responded to the lack of a unique class member in the *Xs → a X* preparations: when the testing was modified somewhat in the imitations with expansions task, again even the youngest group showed a very exact discrimination.

Developmentally, two major changes were discovered. The three-year-old children failed to make egocentric definite responses in great number. But their general response to the systematic stories was too indefinite in general. Their less definite reference was attributed to a slightly weaker referential and representational competence. The indefiniteness largely disappeared under conditions which gave more support to their comprehensional processes, in the imitations with expansions, indicating that the difficulty is not a severe one. The adjacent developmental group, 4 Low, had the competence required to give definite expressions where required. But they made many errors of an egocentric type, giving many definite expressions when a unique member of the nominated class had not been established in the conversation for both themselves and their listeners. The most advanced developmental group, 4 High, were found to be largely free from all errors in their responses.

7
Results from the miscellaneous stories; other analyses

The major results obtained from the stories have been discussed in chapter 6. Two disconnected problems comprise the subject matter of this rather appendicial chapter. In the first section I discuss evidence which confirms that different question phrases may differentially elicit definite and indefinite responses. Different stories are also shown to have the same differential eliciting effect, at least for the three-year-olds. As mentioned in chapter 5, the stories also included a brief investigation of children's ability to make definite reference on the basis of entailment. The results of this investigation are set forth in the second section of this chapter.

The effects of the question phrase

One of the methodological difficulties discussed earlier was the difficulty of the differential expectations set up by such question phrases as *what, who, which, which one*. I noted before that because of the possible effects of different phrases, both versions of any systematic story were told with the same question phrase, despite occasional unnaturalness, or possibly even misleading effects. One story, Car—Boat, was given to both the three-year-olds and the four-year-olds to assess the problem more systematically. The Car—Boat story was one in which someone leaving for the jungle had a car or boat to choose between, and the question is about his choice. The answer should be a definite expression, but even adults sometimes give indefinite responses to it, I have found, where the question-phrase is *what*. I do not really have any well-developed notions as to why this is so. But given that the answer is less determinate than in other stories, the Car—Boat story seemed like a promising one with which to investigate the effect of the question phrase more systematically. The story was told once to each child. Half were asked for the man's choice with the question 'Which one did he use?' and half were asked 'What did he use?'

The results are straightforward, and are displayed in table 7.1. Both age groups gave more definite expressions as answers when the question phrase was 'which one', a reliable overall difference ($x^2 = 5.25$, with Yates' correction, $p < 0.05$). The four-year-olds, as might be expected, produced more definite expressions in each condition. The effect of the question phrase was nevertheless identical for both age groups.

Which one and *what*, then, may already signal to preschool children differential expectations on the part of the speaker as to the expected definiteness of the answer. The result points up the subtlety of the discourse information children may early acquire. It justifies as well the earlier decision to use an identical question phrase in the contrasting versions of each systematic story.

Variation among stories

More generally, it is likely that whole stories may somehow elicit different base-lines of definite response. To take an isolated example, the systematic story Knock Over was a story, like Car—Boat, that asked the child to choose an object that was acted on. Like Car—Boat, the question phrase employed to elicit an answer was *what*. Yet in the *a X → the X* version, Knock Over elicited six definite expressions out of nine responses from the three-year-olds, compared to zero of eight elicited from the same group by the Car—Boat story. In fact, the Cave story, theoretically an *Xs → a X* paradigm, received six definite responses out of fourteen answers from the three-year-olds.

These examples could be given in isolated form at some length. They all indicate the same conclusion: different stories may differ in their base-lines of elicited definite response, and a true test of competence requires stories told in minutely contrasted conditions. I have attempted

Table 7.1. *Effects of different question phrases on answers*

Question	Four-year olds		Three-year-olds	
Phrase	*The X*	*A X*	*The X*	*A X*
Which one	8	1	4	4
What	4	4	0	8

to make a more systematic evaluation of these effects with both age groups, using the results from the systematic stories. For this analysis, a response was scored for its definiteness relative to the answer appropriate to the story version. A definite response to an indefinite-eliciting story version was scored + 1.0, an indefinite response to a definite-eliciting version was scored − 1.0, and accurate answers were scored as 0.0, since their definiteness matched that of the appropriate answer. By this procedure a story that elicited too many indefinites receives a negative score. Missing responses were also scored as 0.0. With subject number 2 (who answered only one story) deleted from the analysis, just 12 per cent of the scores were missing responses.

The analysis indicates that for the three-year-olds, there were indeed reliable differences in definiteness of answers to different stories, $F(6,108) = 3.37, p < 0.01$. The stories are listed in table 7.2 in descending order of the three-year-olds' definiteness of response to them. I have also listed some characteristics of each story: the grammatical role of the questioned reference (e.g. in Looking For, the child is asked 'Who came running out', in which *Who* is a grammatical subject; in Like, the question was 'Which does {he, she} like more?' where *Which* is a grammatical object), and the animacy of the reference and the question phrase used.

There was clearly a substantial range of definiteness among the stories. There are perhaps too many uncontrolled differences among the stories in plot and so on to place much emphasis on the effects of the listed factors (grammatical role, question word, animacy), but some of the regularities in the data are conspicuous. The three stories receiving the most definite responses all contained grammatical subjects as

Table 7.2. *The definiteness of the systematic stories*

Title of story	Question word	Grammatical role	Animacy	Definiteness[a]
Looking For	who	subject	animate	+0.07
Out to Meet	who	subject	animate	0.00
Making Noise	who	subject	animate	0.00
Knock Over	what	object	inanimate	−0.11
Like	which	object	animate	−0.12
Give	what	object	animate	−0.22
Pond	what	object	animate	−0.50

[a]Definiteness computed as definiteness score according to procedure in text divided by total number of responses the score is based on.

questioned reference. Semantically, all three of these grammatical subjects were also agents, the animate instigators of an action. The questioned references of the bottom four stories were all grammatical objects, and mostly the recipients of action. The top three stories are also ones in which the question phrase is the definite-suggesting form *who*. The bottom two stories contained an animate reference questioned for by *what*. In these stories, all of the questioned animates except for those in Make a Noise are animals. It is always difficult, in fact, to know how to refer to animals. If one uses *what* to ask about a human, it is only to ask for specification of what-kind-of-person, not which person. One cannot say 'What did this?' to mean a human, but it is possible to ask 'What is he?' to find out 'He is a doctor' or 'He is a fool.' Referring to animals in the question with *what* may have biased many of the younger children towards the indefinite answering appropriate to the 'What kind of thing was it?' question. These factors are all confounded in the construction of the stories, of course, though they could be systematically assessed, as was the difference between *what* and *which one* in the Car—Boat story. The major thrust of the analysis, though, is straightforward. The stories differed among themselves quite clearly in the base-line of definite responding. Testifying to the more generally stable response of the four-year-olds, no significant variability was found when the same analysis was performed on their answers $(F(6,114) = 1.02, p > 0.25)$.

Investigation of entailment

As will be recalled, just one story was employed in the investigation of children's ability to make entailed definite reference, a story called *Barking*. The child was told of two animals who were playing together, one of which barked and one of which meowed. The child was told that one of them ran away, and asked 'Who ran away?' The answer should be an entailed definite expression — *the dog* or *the cat*.

Fifteen of the four-year-olds gave usable responses. (The other children did not fail to comprehend the story. But they in fact felt compelled to name the animal — 'It's a dog' or 'It's a cat', then said immediately 'The dog ran away' or 'The cat ran away.' The entailment story, of course, establishes class memberships by description. These four-year-olds wanted to identify the class membership explicitly before continuing the story.) Of the fifteen children who immediately answered the question of who ran away, fourteen gave appropriate definite expressions. These responses show a good understanding of entailment by the four-year-olds.

The results from asking the three-year-olds are more equivocal. One girl acted like the four-year-olds who named the animal first, then immediately said 'The dog ran away.' Aside from her, sixteen children answered immediately with simple noun phrases. Of these, nine gave definite responses and seven gave indefinites.

Nine of sixteen does not differ from chance, but random responding may not provide the proper standard against which to compare the results. Probably the closest contrast is provided by the story described earlier as $\emptyset \rightarrow a\ X$, in which the preparation establishes the existence of a referent, but gives it no class description beyond that of *animal*. Here the child was told the characters of a story saw an animal, and asked 'What did they see?' or told that an animal came running out at the characters, and asked 'Who came running out?' Fourteen children were asked the latter story, in which, like the Barking story, the questioned referent is asked for with *who*, is a grammatical subject, and situationally a running animal. Thirteen of these fourteen responses were indefinite noun phrases, while just one was definite. Twelve children in particular answered both the entailment question and the latter version of the $\emptyset \rightarrow a\ X$ story. Eight of these properly gave a definite response to the entailment story and an indefinite answer to the $\emptyset \rightarrow a\ X$ story, while four gave indefinite answers to both. The $\emptyset \rightarrow a\ X$ story, however, failed to provide a completely minimal contrast to the Barking story in one respect. While the entailment stories required a choice between two possibilities (dog or cat), in answering the $\emptyset \rightarrow a\ X$ story, the child was free to choose any animal he wished. On the whole, I think the results indicate that even three-year-olds may have some competence in the use of entailment to prepare a definite reference. But the lack of results from a perfectly contrastive story to the Barking story makes it impossible to ground this assertion securely.

8
Games

A description of the tests

The major point of the games procedure was to investigate more directly children's possible difficulties with non-egocentric reference. In the various stories procedures we found a good deal of consistently egocentric responses in the 4 Low group, and it was assumed that the 3-year-olds only failed to refer egocentrically because of other difficulties with the task, especially the difficulties of establishing specific reference for themselves in a task as abstract as the stories. It may show something of the more indirect investigatory nature of the stories that such intricate analyses and explanations of the groups' responses were necessary. The games procedure provided an opportunity for children to talk about concrete referents, and at the same time provided a more convincing instantiation of egocentric and non-egocentric reference. In the games procedure the children produced definite and indefinite expressions in order to request real toys. Their asking was always part of a larger enterprise, a game in which they participated, and playing with toys was a central aspect of the procedure.

The basic paradigm

The child was to choose a toy to play with from an array of toys from two classes. On half of the occasions, there was just one toy of each type, perhaps a boy and a girl, to choose from. Here the child's answer should more often have been a definite expression, *the boy* or *the girl*. On other occasions, more than one toy of each type was to be chosen from, perhaps three boys and three girls. Here, even if the child should fix one of them in his mind, his listener (me) would not know which one he meant. Thus the situation entailed that the proper response on the child's part was an indefinite reference, unless he could describe the toy he wanted exactly enough, say as 'the boy with brown hair'. The toys were chosen so that simple definite expressions like *the boy* would be improper references.

In playing the games, a second important variable was also employed: the visibility of the toys. On half of the occasions of his choice, the child could actually see the toys he was choosing from. But the other half of the time, the toys were hidden. The idea here is quite straightforward. Imagine a relatively egocentric child faced with choosing a member from the multi-membered sets in each of the two conditions of visibility. When the toys are visible, he could sometimes focus perceptually on one particular member of the group as his choice. His reference to that toy would then be specific for himself, and, should he not take into account that his listener cannot tell what toy is meant from the description, is likely to be a definite expression, such as *the boy*. When the toys are hidden, he can no longer focus perceptually on an individual member of the multi-member sets. Assume the child has the basic semantic competence to refer to any member of a set with an indefinite expression. The child should then do so, for no member of the set can gain a unique status when all members have lost perceptual individuality through having been hidden.

The tests also serve indirectly as a test of the stability of definite reference. When just one member of each class is known to be available, a definite expression should be used whether the toy is out of sight or not. In either visibility condition, the member is quite unique in its class, for listener and speaker alike.

We shall see that each of these problems — referring non-egocentrically when toys are present, referring definitely when toys are absent — causes some difficulty to some of the subjects, the former causing more. But first we need more detailed descriptions of the actual games and procedures.

Description of the games

Down the Hill
Down the Hill was played with a wooden hill, a car, and Fisher-Price toy boys and girls which fit conveniently into the cars. The child sat across from the experimenter at a round table. The hill, the car on top of the hill, and the toys were all placed on the experimenter's side of the table out of the child's reach. The child was told that the experi-

menter would send the car down the hill with a toy child in the car, and the child was to select a toy, one at a time, to be placed in the car. After the child had selected a toy doll for the car, it was rolled down the hill, which slanted towards the child. The child got to catch the car as it rolled across the table to him, or catch it at the ʰottom of the hill, as many of the children liked to do.

I presented the toys, naming them, e.g. 'Here are a boy and girl we can use' or the like. When eliciting the child's request for a toy, I would ask 'Would you like one of those?' if any prompting was needed. If further prompting was needed, the child was then asked 'Who shall we give a ride to now?' In the Down the Hill game, the question word for the prompt was always *who*, and the case was always indirect object.

Feeding the Dragon
In this game the child wore a rather large red rubber dragon puppet on his hand. The dragon had a rather large, openable mouth into which smaller plastic animals could be fitted. Again the child sat across the table from the experimenter, and the toys to be chosen from were on the experimenter's side of the table, out of easy reach. The child was told that the dragon liked to eat animals and asked if he would like to help feed the dragon. The child had to ask for animals for the dragon to eat, one at a time from the toys at the opposite side of the table. As in the Down the Hill game, the toys were initially presented and named. The first prompt used was 'Would he like one of those?' and the second 'What would the dragon like, then?' After the dragon had 'eaten' an animal, the animal was put into one of several colored wooden boxes near the child, as part of the game.

These games generally held the children's interest quite success-fully. All of the children seemed to enjoy playing Down the Hill, and about half asked to play it after it had been played the second time (see chapter 3, Introduction to the Overall Experimental Design). The Dragon game appeared a little less successful. A few children did not like it much or became bored with it, at least from appearances, and only a few asked to play it again after the second play period devoted to it.

Presenting hidden toys
Hidden toys were not visible to the child when he made his choice. Again, I named what toys were available to be chosen from, saying

'There's another boy and girl back here' or whatever was appropriate. The toys were hidden behind the wooden hill when Down the Hill was being played, and hidden behind a large box when the game was Feeding the Dragon. The child was shown the toys before they were hidden in half of the game periods, while in the other half, the toys were hidden without his seeing them. No differences in the outcomes appear to have resulted from this procedural manipulation, and no future reference to it will be made.

Character and placement of the toys
All of the toys of a set were distinguishable from one another. For example, the boys of a set of three boys would differ in hair color, cap color, and wooden body color; or ducks that were used in the Dragon Game would differ in size and color from one another. When seeing completely identical members of a set, it is not completely un-reasonable to refer to them somehow as a single member replicated; 'Give me the boy' when looking at three identical boys is not clearly incorrect. We commonly refer this way ourselves to standardized commercial products like records or identical articles of clothing.

The members of a multiple-membered set were always placed right next to each other, so that the child could see clearly that more than one was present. If the toys were spaced far apart, or if members of different sets were interspersed among each other, the child might not perceive that more than one of each kind was present. Then a definite expression would result not from a failure to apply referential rules correctly, but from simple misinformation. In pilot work, by asking children about the arrays, I was able to determine that this procedure made it quite easy for the child to notice that there was more than one of a kind. Also, of course, when naming the toys I always made reference to the fact that more than one was present, e.g. 'Here are some boys and girls we can use.'

Preventing pointing
These procedures are reasonable ones for evaluating competence if the child constrains his referring to expressions of the form *article + noun*. One can use a definite expression to ask for one out of many boys, if the description is rich enough to make the reference clear, e.g. 'the boy with the blue hat' when only one boy has a blue hat. This kind of elaborated reference was so rare (four responses of a total of around

six hundred) that it caused no difficulty. A more severe difficulty was preventing children from pointing. A perfectly reasonable way of making reference to a particular class member is to point to it and say something that would otherwise be an improper reference, such as 'the boy', 'him', 'this one', or nothing at all. A large number of the children naturally wanted to use this efficient means of making reference. They were prevented from pointing in the following way. I first waited to see if a child was a pointer. (No answer using a point was considered correct or used in scoring.) If the child did point, he was asked not to. If he continued to point, he was told about another part of the game: both he and I were to put our hands on our heads and keep them there until the child had made his request. Many children whose pointing had to be restrained by this technique became accustomed to not pointing, and so the technique could be discontinued. A few others, however, had to play games this way all through the games periods.

Distribution of the tests

Three major factors entered into the design of the games. There were two conditions of the number of toys presented in each class, singular (one of each) or plural (more than one of each, usually three). There were two conditions of visibility of toys, visible and invisible. And finally, there were two games, Down the Hill and Feeding the Dragon. The result is a matrix of eight possible combinations of conditions. Each child played both of the games in each of the four conditions of number and visibility. The eight conditions were split up among the four games periods (see chapter 3, Introduction to the Overall Experimental Design) so that in each period, the child played just one game (Down the Hill or Feeding the Dragon) in just one condition of number (singular or plural). He first played the game with the toys visible, and then played the same game with new toys that were hidden. Here is an example of the order in which one child received the various conditions:

> *Session 1*
> Period 1: Down the Hill, plural; visible then invisible.
> Period 2: Feeding the Dragon, singular; visible then Invisible.
>
> *Session 2*
> Period 3: Dragon, plural; visible then invisible.
> Period 4: Down the Hill, singular; visible then invisible.

The invisible condition always followed the visible condition because in pilot testing, I found that it was often difficult to explain the game and how it was to be played when the toys were hidden; with the toys visible to the child the problem diminished considerably. The fact that choices of hidden toys always followed choosing visible ones could have caused difficulties in comparing the results from the visible and invisible conditions. In discussing the results, I shall discuss evidence that the lack of counterbalancing did not in fact lead to any serious analytic problems.

As with the other procedures, a single design was made up for twenty subjects and repeated for each age group. Each game, number, and visibility condition appeared equally often in each of the four games periods throughout the two sessions. Details of the design are to be found in appendix ix.

The results of testing
Initial analysis

Method of scoring
Each child was tested in eight conditions. In each of these conditions I endeavored to obtain a minimum of two usable responses from each child, and was generally successful. The child's score was simply his accuracy, based on a maximum of the two initial responses for each child. If a child gave no responses in a condition (refusing to play the game, or articleless answers), his score was filled in by the mean of the age and sex group for that condition, corrected by the child's own accuracy in conditions for which his scores were available.

Overall accuracy of each group
In order to estimate the overall accuracies of the different age and sex groups, each child was given a score comprised of the average of his scores in each of the eight conditions. These results are summarized in table 8.1. All four age-sex groups displayed well over change performance. The only group that appears distinctively different from the others is the four-year-old girls, who answered with outstandingly high accuracy.

A full analysis of the results from the study requires considering five variables: number (singular versus plural); visibility (visible versus

Table 8.1. *Accuracies for games*

Group	Accuracy, with 95% C.I.	Test for difference from chance	
		t	p
3-year-old boys	0.72 ± 0.09	$t(9) = 4.56$	$p < 0.002$
3-year-old girls	0.76 ± 0.09	$t(9) = 5.87$	$p < 0.001$
4-year-old boys	0.76 ± 0.08	$t(9) = 6.88$	$p < 0.001$
4-year-old girls	0.92 ± 0.07	$t(9) = 11.67$	$p < 0.001$

invisible); game (Down the Hill versus Feeding the Dragon); age (three-year-olds versus four-year-olds); and sex (girls versus boys). It is statistically not difficult to analyze the results in terms of all of these variables at once; but the resulting analysis becomes quite difficult to discuss, and many important results are obscured. Consequently, I shall adopt the strategy here of discussing the analysis for smaller groups of subjects, rather than attempting a detailed comment on the complete set.

Analysis of the four-year-olds

Sex differences in performance
For the first time in these studies, a substantial sex difference in accuracy was obtained. The girls were reliably more accurate than the boys, $F(1, 18) = 8.067$, $p < 0.01$. The girls' accuracy was 0.92, and a separate analysis shows that neither the kind of game played, the visibility of the toys, or the number of referents to be chosen from had any effect on how accurately they responded. Their competence as a group was very nearly perfect. There is presently little more to say about how the girls played the games, and I shall devote the remaining analysis of the four-year-olds' results to discussing the performance of the four-year-old boys.

Analysis for the four-year-old boys

Egocentric responding
We saw earlier that overall the boys showed well over chance performance. When only one toy of each kind was present they made their requests with definite noun phrases far more often than when more than one toy of each kind was available. But this does not tell us about how they performed under different conditions of visibility and

number. Their accuracies in each of the number and visibility conditions is summarized briefly below:

	Singular	*Plural*
Visible	0.75	0.54
Invisible	0.77	0.89

As can be seen, when there was just one toy of each type to be chosen from, the boys' accuracy was around 0.75, whether the toys were visible or not. But when more than one toy was present (number = plural), visibility became quite important. When the toys were visible, nearly half of the responses were egocentric definite expressions. The child would see a group of boys and girls, and ask for 'the boy'. Hiding the toys dropped the proportion of these incorrect definite expressions to just 0.11. The effect is a reliable one (for the interaction of number and visibility, $F(1,9) = 10.974$, $p < 0.01$) and accords well with the predicted pattern of egocentric responding. When the toys were visible, a child could selectively attend to one of them. He would then sometimes use a definite expression to refer to the toy he had focused on, even though the listener could not tell which one was meant. Seven of the ten boys referred egocentrically in this way at least half of the time. In contrast, no particular toy could be attended to when the toys were hidden. The children only knew that more than one of each kind was present. They accordingly asked for no particular member of one of the classes with an indefinite expression. The fact that definiteness of responding was not similarly affected when toys were just one of a kind supports this analysis. Clearly it was not just a random shift of definiteness of response that caused the boys to use more definites when many toys of each kind were visible than when they were not.

Subjectively, it was sometimes clear that the child had a particular toy in mind. He would seem to be staring intently at one, or even occasionally, after I had chosen one of the toys, say 'That's the one', or 'That one's all right, I guess.' (It was usually a good guess that when Down the Hill was being played, if the child wanted one toy in particular, it was the one placed nearer the car.)

Competence in response
The boys' answers did show some command of the difference between the number conditions, quite clearly so when the toys were invesible.

The difference in how many definite expressions were used for the different conditions of number obviously dropped when the toys were visible. Even here most of the boys differentiated in the proper direction however, and the overall group performance still exceeded chance when the toys were visible, $t(9) = 2.50$, $p < 0.05$. I shall return later to the problems of interpreting this result, since it also appears in the three-year-olds' analyses.

An effect of the games

The game that was being played did not reliably affect the overall accuracy of the boys' requests. But the four-year-old boys did give more definite expressions as answers when playing Down the Hill than when playing Feeding the Dragon. As a result, their responses were more accurate when number was singular, and answers should have been definite expressions; conversely, their answers were less accurate when number was plural, and an indefinite expression was appropriate (for the interaction of game and number, $F(1, 9) = 6.97$, $p < 0.05$). The result resembles that found earlier for the three-year-olds' performance with stories, where it was found that different stories had different base-lines of definiteness in elicited response. Again it is possible to advance suggestions as to why the difference should have occurred: the asked-for toy in the Down the Hill game was an agent, while the toy was an object of action in the Feeding the Dragon game; the Down the Hill game seemed to arouse and maintain interest more successfully, which should increase attention to the toys as particular individuals of their class. But none of these suggestions is more than tentative.

Analysis for the three-year-olds

Sex differences in games

The two sexes did not differ in overall accuracy, $F(1, 18) = 0.429$, $p > 0.25$. A rather peculiar effect was obtained, however. The four-year-old boys, it will be recalled, responded with more definite expressions to Down the Hill than to Feeding the Dragon. Like them, the three year-old girls gave more definite expressions as responses to Down the Hill in all conditions, though responding with equal overall accuracy to both games. In contrast, the three-year-old boys gave the same proportion of definite expressions in playing both games (0.41 and 0.43

for Down the Hill and Feeding the Dragon respectively). I have charted the effect, which is reliable ($F(1, 18) = 6.73, p < 0.05$), in figure 8.1. Aside from this difference in the baseline of definiteness in playing the two games, no other sex-associated effects were found among the three-year-olds. The results is a puzzling one, but it seems unimportant, and so I continue the analysis of the three-year-olds as a single group.

Main analyses
Accuracy turned out to be affected by a complex combination of the factors of game, number, and visibility ($F(1, 18) = 10.556, p < 0.01$). These effects may be disentangled optimally by a consideration of the important results for each game separately. The children's accuracies in playing each game in each condition may be found in table 8.2. In playing Down the Hill, the three-year-olds responded very much as the four-year-old boys did in playing both games. Competence in referring to singular objects was identical when objects were present or hidden; about 75 per cent of the answers, correctly, were definite expressions. In contrast, when more than one toy of each kind was present, visibility affected responses very strongly. When the toys were in sight, the three-year-olds asked for a toy correctly with an indefinite expression just 58 per cent of the time; 42 per cent of their responses were erroneous definite expressions. When the toys were hidden,

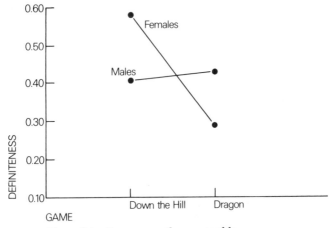

Figure 8.1   Sex x game, three-year-olds

accuracy rose to 93 per cent. Presumably, once again, when the toys were visible, the child could focus on a particular toy and request it egocentrically with a definite expression. After the toys were hidden, bringing a particular toy into focus in this way became impossible: nearly all of the requests were indefinite expressions presumably made in reference to the notion of any member of the class.

A more peculiar effect was obtained when the three-year-olds played Feeding the Dragon. Once again, responding to many-membered sets became more accurate after the toys were hidden. But the number of indefinite expressions also increased markedly when just one toy of each kind was hidden. As a result, accuracy in asking for singular toys dropped from 0.76 when the toys were visible to just 0.39 when the toys were absent. I do not know of any convincing explanation for why indefinite responses should have increased in both the singular and plural conditions after the toys were hidden in playing Feeding the Dragon. No general appeal can be made to the effects of making the toys invisible; when the three-year-olds played Down the Hill, indefiniteness increased only in the plural condition. It may be that the form of the prompt for Feeding the Dragon (question phrase = *what* to refer to animals) or the semantic role of the requested toy (object of action) were influential when the toys were not concretely present. We have already seen how these factors may be determinative of the manner of answering in earlier chapters. Or the increase in indefiniteness might be caused by some more general factor, such as loss of interest in the game, causing the children to pay less attention to the particular referents used in the game. I noted earlier that interest

Table 8.2. *The three-year-olds' accuracies in the different number conditions of the games*

Game = Down the Hill		
Visibility	Number = singular	Number = plural
Toys visible	0.75	0.58
Toys hidden	0.76	0.93

Game = Feeding the Dragon		
Visibility	Number = singular	Number = plural
Toys visible	0.76	0.74
Toys hidden	0.39	0.93

in Feeding the Dragon was less than in Down the Hill. These all can only be completely *ad hoc* suggestions, needless to say.

The lack of counterbalancing of visibility and invisibility

In playing the games, the children always played with visible toys to ask for before requesting hidden ones. An interpretive difficulty accordingly arises: the differences between responses to visible versus invisible toys could have been caused by some more general shift of responding in the course of each game period, rather than being caused by particular differences between having the toys visible or invisible. A crucial result obtained from the games was that the number of indefinite responses in the plural condition increased when the referents were hidden. But if indefinite expressions simply became more common as playing a game proceeded in any period, the shift could be clearly interpreted. Or if responses became more accurate in the course of each games period, the same difficulty would arise.

The data do not seriously support these counter hypotheses. The shift towards more indefinite responding was not general throughout except in one instance: the three-year-olds' playing of Feeding the Dragon. The four-year-old boys gave more indefinite answers when multi-membered sets were hidden, but not when single-membered sets were concealed; similarly for the three-year-olds' responses to Down the Hill. The results support the hypothesis of egocentric responding clearly, but are inexplicable from a hypothesis of generally increasing indefiniteness.

Similarly, no general increase in accuracy occurred throughout the tests. In asking for singular objects, children's accuracy remained identical when the toys were hidden, except in the case of the three-year-olds playing Feeding the Dragon, in which case it decreased. I conclude that the failure to counterbalance visibility–invisibility orders does not impair the interpretation of the game findings.

Competence in specific and non-specific reference

The responses of all age groups to the hidden toys displayed once again the children's competence in dealing with the specific–non-specific distinction. Below are given the proportions of definite expressions given by the three- and four-year-olds when the toys were hidden:

	THREE-YEAR-OLDS	
	Down the Hill	*Feeding the Dragon*
Singular	0.75	0.39
Plural	0.07	0.06

	FOUR-YEAR-OLDS	
	Down the Hill	*Feeding the Dragon*
Singular	0.91	0.79
Plural	0.10	0.10

Clearly, asking for any member of the invisible set with an indefinite expression caused little difficulty to the children at any age. This result corresponds well to the children's early established competence in understanding and making references to any member of a set, as verified both naturalistically and in earlier experimental results. The four-year-olds are better at giving definite expressions where required, but both groups clearly distinguished by giving more definite expressions to ask for a unique class member than to ask for one out of many. The results buttress earlier ones in demonstrating children's command of the specific–non-specific dimension when referents are not concretely visible.

Egocentric responding

The above results are of interest, but what was central to the games procedures was the way in which a clear demonstration of egocentric response could be obtained in the contrast between responses to the visible and hidden toys. All groups in the study, with the exception of the four-year-old girls, displayed some amount of egocentric responding (though of course individual members of the other groups referred quite accurately). In particular, the fact that the three-year-olds gave many egocentric responses supports the hypothesis that their general failure to do so in the stories tasks was caused by their lack of imagination more than a non-egocentric competence. Making the referents visible brought about relatively high levels of egocentric response.

It is of some interest to inspect the responses of the two four-year-old groups defined by imitations, 4 Low and 4 High. The 4 High group did in fact give fewer egocentric responses, defined as definite expressions given when more than one of each kind of toy was visible. Their error

rate was 0.16, as compared to 0.42 to the 4 Low group, a reliable difference, $t(18) = 2.16, p < 0.05$. Thus competence in imitations was mildly predictive of competence in the games test as well, although sex was even more predictive.

A last problem

Although egocentricity of response seems clearly demonstrated by these procedures and results, there is a residual problem. All groups gave more indefinite expressions when asking for a single referent out of a group than when just one of a kind was present, even when referents were visible. Do these correct indefinites show some knowledge of taking into account the listener's point of view? Or did the children sometimes look at a group of referents and simply not bother to focus on one, so asking for any member of the class? Either of these might be responsible for the differentiation. The problem here is a more general one that will be discussed in the final chapter.

Summary

Children were given tests in which they requested a toy to play with, from arrays which were either visible or invisible, and in which toys were either one or more than one of a kind. They gave definite expressions and indefinite expressions differentially, depending on the number of members in each class, both when toys were visible and hidden. All groups but the four-year-old girls, however, gave more incorrect definites to ask for one toy out of many when the toys were visible. This was taken as indicating that when the toys were visible, the children often selectively attended to one of the set, making reference to it specific for themselves. When this was combined with a failure to take into account the lack of knowledge of the experimenter, incorrect definite reference then occurred. Different effects were also obtained in the two different games played, with results for Down the Hill in general being more consistent with the hypothesis initially offered.

9

General discussion; problems in adult response

Children's knowledge of specificity and non-specificity

In the framework adopted at the beginning of this book, the system of definite and indefinite articles depends on competence in the use of two semantic factors. The first of these was specificity or non-specificity of reference, the distinction between referring to a class member with a unique specification that distinguishes the member from all other members, versus making reference to a referent marked only by the class membership of the referring phrase, or making reference only to the idea of a class member. The second factor of importance was the consideration of whether a reference specific for oneself would make correspondingly specific reference for the listener: whether the listener could identify the reference as being to just the particular class member intended by the speaker.

Our results give a relatively unproblematical evaluation of what young children know about the specificity–non-specificity dimension. Brown's naturalistic analyses (1973) indicated children's competence in making this distinction in naturalistic situations. In a large number of experimentally created circumstances, varying in the abstractness and awkwardness of the referential situation, we have similarly found that even the knowledge of children who had not been using articles long generalized far beyond the limited circumstances of more natural usage. Results from the comprehension tests of chapter 4 indicate that children early understand that definite expressions refer to class members already made prominent in a conversational context, and indefinite expressions in the same context make reference to some non-conspicuous member. As shown in the stories which contrasted $a\ X \rightarrow a\ X$ and $a\ X \rightarrow the\ X$ paradigms, children early understand the difference between indefinite expressions which actually make reference to a particular class member as opposed to those which do not. In a more active 'comprehension' task, imitations with expansions, children had clear ideas on whether someone else should use a definite expression to refer to an object, depending on the referent's previous uniqueness or lack of it for themselves. They could produce indefinite expressions to refer generically (Like story, chapter 6) or to ask for 'any member' of a class (systematic stories, hidden condition in games). In minimally contrastive conditions they were able to make definite reference to unique class members.

Of course, we must note some initial instability, particularly in the younger children's use of definite expressions. These difficulties, as shown in the imitations with expansions procedure, are not indissolubly connected with reference to non-concrete class members. I think much of their difficulty was caused by a competing tendency, to refer indefinitely on being asked to choose a class identify for a referent (cf. chapter 6 for discussion of this point). Difficulties in making definite reference seemed constantly to be associated in particular with situations in which the child was asked 'What ...' about an animal. In the games procedure, it was Feeding the Dragon that always elicited more indefinites when a distinction appeared between the games, and the problem has been discussed more extensively in chapter 7 for the Stories. Even when these difficulties arose, the distinction between specific and non-specific reference remained a reliable one.

Implications of early specific—non-specific competence

The fact that specific—non-specific competence could be found throughout such a wide variety of contexts supports the hypothesis that the abstract linguistic dimension employed in our descriptions actually has early psychological reality as one along which the children's understanding of articles is organized. The child truly must interpret the relatively limited experience he has in how the articles are used in a more abstract, generalizable fashion, or extension of the distinction to the wide range of referential contexts represented by these studies would elude him. The degree of widespread competence to be found in these young children, particularly the group under three-and-a-half, is remarkable. We saw earlier that specific and non-specific reference are connected in no clear way with external physical attributes or relations of perceived objects. Rather the child must monitor the state of representations of class members, or the idea of one, in his own conceptual processing; he must connect these abstract representations with some very slight phonological sounds, *a* and *the*, in order to attain proper usage. Bierwisch (1970) has proposed that all 'semantic structures might finally be reduced to components representing the basic dispositions of the cognitive and perceptual structure of the human organism (p. 181). In the present case we can see straightforwardly how complex some of the 'basic dispositions of the cognitive and perceptual structure' required by ordinary linguistic usage may be, and correspondingly the complexity of the mental functioning of the young child. As described in chapter 1, Piaget (1962) has written that 'the child at this state achieves neither true generality nor true individuality, the notions he uses fluctuating incessantly between the two extremes (p. 224). Similarly, Bruner *et al.* (1966) have discussed how the young child's representations may be heavily dependent on iconic, imagic representations for symbolic storage. The results obtained in study point, on the contrary, to well-developed early referential and representational abilities. It is difficult to conceive how children whose representations incessantly fluctuate between true generality and true individuality, or depend heavily on imagic representation, could so successfully formulate and use the abstract referential dimension of specificity and non-specificity. In order to make the requisite referential distinctions, children must not only possess well-differentiated notions of individual and general class membership, but be able to process these notions recursively for use in the linguistic system.

Accounting for semantic acquisition
One of the problems that we cannot deal with at all adequately at the present time is the process by which children come to associate these more abstract conceptual dimensions, such as specificity–non-specificity, with the particular linguistic means used to express them. The difficulty is a more general one for explaining all language acquisitional processes. The child's task is always to formulate a relation between the meaningful contexts, both verbal and non-verbal, in which a group of physical sounds appear, and the meaningful use of the word or construction represented linguistically by those sounds. It is easy to forget that the child, to the best of our present knowledge, does not have an extensive corpus of data at any one time with which to work. He probably cannot record numerous large stretches of conversation

and all of the contextual information that accompanied them, as can an adult linguist investigating a novel language. It is not likely that he remembers, for example, any large number of the particular instances in which *the* or *a* preceded a noun and the contexts in which the class member denoted by the noun appeared. Quite possibly the child must formulate initial guesses about the meanings of such abstract morphemes as the articles on the basis of just a few instances of use. These initial guesses can be further compared to other instances he hears for checking or revision, but again it is improbable that the child begins work anew with a large store of sentences and contexts at his disposal. In the case of concrete objects such quick formulation of meanings strikes one as less formidable, though still a considerable one given all the different classes in which a given referent may participate. (A table, for example, may be *furniture, brown, table, wood, flat*, and so on.) When the reference is comparatively abstract, as it is for articles and a multitude of other morphemes, the problem becomes even more striking. The fact that children's relatively early formulations of the use of articles extend as widely as they do gives evidence that they can quickly formulate abstract, generalizable semantic principles of usage for the morphemes they hear. McNeill (1970) and others (e.g. Anglin, 1970) have contrasted what seems to be the quick acquisition of syntactic structures in early years to the slower acquisition of lexical semantics. Further work probably will demonstrate that semantic acquisitions do increase in quantity for years after the preschool period; considering the conceptual complexity of many of the words that children (and adults) eventually acquire, words acquired after the preschool period will probably turn out to be qualitatively more complex in important ways. But I think that with careful investigation, we shall also find that semantic acquisitions of great analytic complexity take place with unexpected quickness and facility in the earlier years as well, under difficult acquisitional circumstances.

Problems of estimating non-egocentric competence

Egocentric reference

What is more dubious is the child's early ability to take into account his listener's ability to place uniquely the reference of the child's definite expressions. The results of this study indicate a rather slowly growing competence, consonant with results from other studies (e.g.

Piaget, 1955). Just four three-year-olds and eleven four-year-olds gave no more than one erroneous definite response in playing the games and stories, and simultaneously gave definite expressions where required at least three-quarters of the time (this last requirement is necessary so as not to overcredit children who were simply generally rather indefinite).

These evaluations are based, naturally,. on experimental evidence. The mistakes found in these tasks, however, do not seem completely isolated. We already know of the many referential errors Brown (1973) found in the three young subjects of his sample. When talking more spontaneously with me and their mothers, children seen in this study also made numerous egocentric errors, especially some three-year-olds. One subject (E.T.), for example, once began and completed a conversation with me by saying 'I gave the pounding thing to Ken.' I was not able to elicit any more information about the identity of the pounding thing or Ken. D.D., asked at the end of the Car–Boat story 'So what did he use?' (referring to the man who chose between a car and a boat) said 'the reindeer'. After I said 'What?' he said 'I have reindeer', apparently meaning some he had at home. A.G. played with an airplane in the first experimental session. Coming back the second time, he suddenly plunged into conversation: 'Well, we don't have any more airplanes because Sashie broke *the other airplane.*' Inaccuracies occurred much less frequently with four-year-olds, but occurred nevertheless with them also, as with K.G., a member of the 4 Low group: 'I went to Jimmy's birthday. He had a five. He was five. I brought him — *the alligator puppet.*' None of the children who according to the experimental tests had more control over these problems made these erroneous references. The presence of naturalistic errors and their fading out over time gives some confidence that the experimentally elicited mistakes did not exist in a vacuum.[1]

1. Also relevant here is the work by Peterson (1974), who had children describe week-old, real-life events and accidents either to the adult who had been there at the time or to an adult who had not witnessed the incidents (see above, p. 12 for further description). Peterson found that both the three- and four-year-old subjects used more indefinites to mention a referent to the unknowledgeable one. The differentiation was far sharper in the four-year-old group, however, and even when they were talking to the naive listener a majority of the articles used by three-year-olds were, incorrectly, definite articles. Peterson also found that even the four-year-old children as a group made numbers of erroneous definite references. These results, from a task which nicely mixes naturalistic and experimental techniques, by and large agree with the results discussed here.

Non-egocentric reference among egocentric children

It remains a fact, however, that non-egocentric indefinite expressions occurred even among children and groups that gave many egocentric definite expressions. The 4 Low group of the stories test consisted of nine children with an overall accuracy of less than 0.50 in responding to $Xs \rightarrow a\ X$ Story situations. Nevertheless, only three of the nine children gave no indefinite expressions at all when telling the $Xs \rightarrow a\ X$ Stories. Similarly, fifteen children playing the games each had accuracies of less than 0.50 when asking for a toy out of visible, multi-membered sets. Only two of these fifteen never gave a correct answer in that condition; each of the rest gave more definites in the singular visible than in the plural visible condition, showing some discrimination.

Anecdotal data also show that even some children who made both experimental and spontaneous egocentric errors also at times introduced referents correctly in naturalistic speech with me and their mothers. D.D. was cited above for his error in responding to the Car—Boat story with 'the reindeer'. When I exclaimed 'What', however, he said 'I have reindeer', which is informative and reasonably appropriate in form. A.G., also cited above, at another time told me 'I saw a squirrel that bites.' Many children introduced referents to me by saying 'I have a X' or 'We have a X', usually inspired by seeing a particular X in the play sessions.

A single factor account

The problem, then, is accounting for non-egocentric references among children who often refer egocentrically. One possible account is that such apparently correct reference is not really based on non-egocentric communicative competence at all, but rather stems from the first, early established semantic factor of specificity for the self. The solution offered for early correct indefinite references here is that the child does not yet really have the class member clearly uniquely represented for himself when he refers to it. Essentially this explanation was given for the low proportion of egocentric errors in the three-year-olds' responses to the $Xs \rightarrow a\ X$ Stories. They lacked the imaginative powers to represent a unique member firmly before responding, since the preparation of the story only informed them that many Xs were present. Similarly, when more than one of each kind of toy was present in playing games, the child may sometimes have scanned them only as a group, without any individual one catching his attention. He would then make his choice with an indefinite expression because he himself has no particular member of the class in mind when choosing. When just one referent of each type was present, the child would naturally make reference that was specific for himself more often.

In the case of children who make egocentric errors in substantial numbers, the plausibility of a single-factor account is not easy to dispute. If one is willing to be somewhat liberal in interpreting when referents might and might not acquire unique representations in the psychological process of making reference, the one factor has considerable explanatory power.

But describing children's competence as governed by only a one factor until perfect referential competence is reached probably constitutes a case of stressing theoretical parsimony too strongly. The combination of some experimental competence with scattered competence shown in spontaneous conversations probably indicates some early imperfect form of non-egocentric reference. In his investigation of how his three subjects learned English, Brown (1973) found that various obligatory morphemes, such as the plural, possessive, and progressive endings (and articles) do not suddenly appear at all times when appropriate in children's acquisition. Rather, their appearance in obligatory contexts becomes more and more probable over time.

If we consider the case of the two factors involved in articles, there is no reason for the same kind of development not to apply. The specific— non-specific dimension, which in the end depends on the child's taking into account his own knowledge of class members and classes, clearly develops relatively early. What probably grows more slowly are procedures and criteria of usage which take into account the state of knowledge of one's listener.

Different models of the development of non-egocentric competence

By referring to non-egocentric competence so broadly, however, we may obscure the developmental possibilities. I shall try now to be more exact in describing the competence and how it might develop. It seems relatively clear what the basic abstract principle behind non-egocentric use of articles is. One thinks of there being a basic semantic notion which would be expressed verbally as something like 'For me to say *the X*, it is necessary that whoever I am talking to must confident-

ly be able to assign a unique reference to *the X*, and that the reference be the same as the one I intend.' Speakers do not consciously have
knowledge of such a principle, of course. But intuitions about how
definite and indefinite expressions should be made can be partly summarized by this kind of abstract requirement, and speakers often act
as though their behavior is shaped by it.

Such knowledge must nonetheless find its application in particular
situations. One needs sub-rules, as I shall call them, for evaluating
whether or not the listener will be able to identify X uniquely. Many
such sub-rules might be employed, of varying specificity and efficiency.
I shall list below examples of possible sub-rules:

> I am pointing at X.
> X is in the same physical context as the listener and myself,
> and is the only X in the context.
> I am talking about household affairs, and there is only one X
> in this household.
> The listener and I saw X together in some circumstances and
> we are talking about those circumstances.
> Everybody knows X (X = the sun, the moon, etc.)
> X has been mentioned in the present conversation.
> X has been brought up (entailed) by something else men-
> tioned in this conversation. (A number of sub-rules are
> needed to determine this.)
> X and my listener are vaguely associated for me somehow. (A
> very poor heuristic, but a common one, I think.)

Let us call each of these sub-rules or indicators R. Then we have:

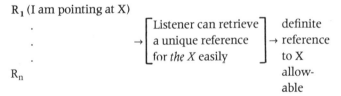

R_1 (I am pointing at X)

$\left. \begin{array}{c} \cdot \\ \cdot \\ \cdot \\ R_n \end{array} \right. \rightarrow \left[\begin{array}{c} \text{Listener can retrieve} \\ \text{a unique reference} \\ \text{for } the \ X \text{ easily} \end{array} \right] \rightarrow \begin{array}{l} \text{definite} \\ \text{reference} \\ \text{to X} \\ \text{allow-} \\ \text{able} \end{array}$

The middle step, 'Listener can retrieve ... ' corresponds to abstract
semantic knowledge which we suppose mediates the connection between $R_1 - R_n$ and the actual behavior of making a definite reference.

The complementary judgement, verbalized by 'Listener cannot retrieve a unique reference for *X*', may be called for by no R_{1-n} being

applicable, or may have positive sub-rules associated with it, such as 'The listener has not heard of X', or in physical contexts, 'The listener is not attending to X presently.' Then X must be introduced into the conversation by some means, perhaps by indefinite reference to it in an appropriate introductory statement ('There's a bug on your head,' 'We saw an enormous dog in the park yesterday') or possibly pointing if this is possible. Such introductions, as discussed in appendix XI, may be optional and elaborate — 'I see you have a new stereo set.'

A First developmental model
Clearly even with a basic command of the basic semantic principle of making non-egocentric references, its application may be a delicate matter, depending as it does on careful attention to situational factors. Even if a child commands the basic semantic principle near the beginning of his use of articles, he might apply this basic knowledge only sporadically because of the possession of only a few sub-rules and primitive means of judging their applicability. With experience and age he would come to formulate finer and more sensitive rules, and simultaneously, with improvement in general attentional, mnemonic, and cognitive factors, come to improve their application. Such a picture of development would look like the following:

Time 1:   Possession of semantic principle, sub-rules R_1-R_i.
Time 2:   Possession of semantic principle, sub-rules R_1-R_k.
          $k > i$ (i.e. he has more sub-rules).
Time 3:   Possession of semantic principle, sub-rules R_1-R_n.
          Etc.

Particular sub-rules might be deleted or refined with age as well. This picture of development assumes a relatively general understanding of the basic semantic principles at an early time, but with a poor ability to apply them. Feedback such as their mothers gave Adam, Eve, and Sarah — 'What cat?' 'What bowl?' — can be expected to aid in sharpening the child's criteria and reminding him of the need to apply them.

A second model
But in fact, in the model of non-egocentric usage posed above, the more abstract semantic principle of non-egocentric reference is a theoretical intermediate, posed on the basis of intuition. A diametrically opposed developmental hypothesis is that in the beginning of correct non-

egocentric usage, correspondences are formed between such sub-rules and behavior directly, without the intermediary non-egocentric abstract semantic principle. Such clusters of sub-rules could exist and grow for some time and lead to non-egocentric usage in some, though not all, situations, before a more general principle was abstracted from them. In such a model, acquisition takes the following course:

Time 1: Sub-rules$_{1-i}$.
Time 2: Sub-rules$_{1-k}$, $k > i$.
Time 3: Non-egocentric principle of use + sub-rules R_1-R_n, $n > k$.

Variations on these alternatives are possible, of course. Sub-rules may again be expected to alter with time. Some well-learned sub-rules might never come under the control of the basic semantic principle; or they might be under such control occasionally, but generally run off automatically. I will not try to devise a model here of what might be called automatic non-egocentric reference, but it is clear that such models, varying in efficiency, sensitivity, and effectiveness can be devised to cover varying ranges of conversational situations. We could expect individuals to differ in the degree to which such automatization is applied, and in the degree to which they could notice exceptions in novel situations, such that new computations became necessary, under the guidance of the general semantic principle.

In fact, perhaps the general principle of non-egocentric usage that we have assumed is only a convenient summary of a collection of referential rules of varying generality that speakers employ. These are general difficulties we face in analyzing what are complex and abstract linguistic and cognitive systems. Once we agree that people formulate and use underlying principles more general than the behaviors they display, it becomes more difficult to analyze the exact nature of human knowledge.

Experimental procedures with adults

The results of these studies clearly do not allow us to choose among these complex developmental alternatives, nor is it clear on an *a priori* basis what kinds of studies would allow such a choice to become a certain one. The complexity of the developmental process can be documented in another way, however, by demonstrating that even the endpoint of development may not be as simply described as we might imagine or desire.

The first experimental procedure

The experiment I shall report here grew out of another attempt to compare the responses of adults and their children. The procedure was designed to insure that the speaker was making a reference that was specific for himself but not for his listener. An opaque screen was placed between the experimenter and the subject. The subject was given a toy plastic car, one of those used earlier in playing Down the Hill and some of the comprehension games, and some small animals: five plastic ducks and four wooden rabbits. He was asked to put one of the animals into the car. Afterwards I asked the subject 'Who got into the car?'

This test, in which the referent was clearly known to the subject but not to me, was intended as a clear demonstration of the relative non-egocentricity of the parents.[1]

Results

In fact, the two groups performed rather similarly. The task is a straight-forward $Xs \rightarrow a \ X$ paradigm, entailing an indefinite expression as the best answer. Ten of the seventeen children who participated referred incorrectly, with a definite expression. But so did seven of the thirteen adults who were tested. There was really no difference between the groups.

Of course, the contrasting case could have been tried, in which just one rabbit and one duck were available to go into the car. Probably all of the adults would have said 'the duck' or 'the rabbit' in this condition, thus showing some group knowledge of the proper contrast. But the rather large number of errors made by the adults appeared more interesting than this particular demonstration of competence.

A second procedure

I wondered whether there might not be a contrasting procedure to display the nature of the erroneous responses more vividly. The follow-ing situation was the closest contrast I was able to devise. Once again

1. Using *who* as a question phrase was no doubt a little unnatural here. But it was employed, for example, in the Cave story that was told to adults and children, which all participating adults answered correctly, as did the 4 High children. (It is interesting that a number of adults remarked on the unnaturalness of the question after they answered the Cave story. A few said they wanted to say something like 'Suzy' in response – i.e. name a particular person in response to 'Who ... ?')

a screen was placed between the experimenter and the subjects. (All of the subjects were randomly chosen parents of children in the study.) In this procedure, however, I had the animals and the car. I showed the toys to the subject, and then put them on my side of the screen. The parent was then told that I was going to put one of the animals into the car. The parent was then asked. 'Who do you think got into the car?' The situation is not an exact adverse of the first, since in both tasks I did the asking. But it is quite close, down to the slightly anomalous use of *who*.

In the first experimental task, then, the subject knew what animal had gotten in and I did not. In the second, I knew and the subject did not. The results are shown below.

	Response = *the X*	Response = *a X*
Parent sees animals (first procedure)	7	6
Parent does not see animal (second procedure)	2	11

The adults made more errors when they had personal knowledge of the particular animal entering the car. An exact test of the results gives $p < 0.09$ (two-tailed) for the difference between conditions. Since then, to round out the numbers a little, I have asked four more middle-class adults to take part in this task, two in each procedure (bringing the number in each condition up to fifteen). One of the two adults who could see the animal described his choice with a definite expression, while both from whom the animals were hidden used indefinite expressions. With fifteen subjects in each condition, $x^2 = 3.75$ (with Yates' correction), $p < 0.06$. The results appear strong enough to cast doubt on the complete security of adult referential competence.

There are other procedures one could attempt in order to clarify the nature of adult errors. Adults could be tested again in the condition in which the toys are on their side of the screen; but rather than asking them directly to say which animal had gotten into the car, one could give them the question and then ask which expression provided a better answer, *a duck* or *the duck*. Adults might then always choose the indefinite expression, which would indicate that their intuitions about a choice between expressions exceeded the accuracy of actual performance.

But the point, if no other, of this last study is that the definiteness favored by the specificity of reference for the self sometimes takes precedence over the indefinite reference specified by the criteria of calculating the listener's knowledge even for adults at various times. Perhaps competence, at least as measured by actual performances of the above kind, never reaches a perfect state. Adults assuredly have firmer command of the use of articles and other non-egocentric communicative competencies than do young children. But a change in referential context, bringing about more concrete knowledge of the referent to the speaker, perhaps resulting in somewhat novel referential circumstances as well (speaking across a screen), elicited errors from adults that theoretically strongly resemble those elicited in earlier described procedures with children. These results make us aware of the multiply-determined basis of linguistic performance, and the need for speaking in fine rather than gross ways of the development of referential abilities.

A final methodological note

In the previous sections I have dicussed two major findings of the present work: the early and apparently general establishment of a specific-non-specific dimension in children's use and understanding of articles; and the more slowly developing and problematical nature of the non-egocentric use of articles. A third problem throughout has been methodological, and effects of different means of testing what is presumably the same underlying competence. On the whole I think that these results, particularly those obtained about the early extent of children's knowledge of specificity versus non-specificity, give cause for optimism about the possibilities of investigating the acquisition of semantics in an experimental fashion. But the relation of experimental techniques to the competencies they measure is clearly a problem (Flavell and Wohlwill, 1969). We have seen how different tasks may shift the base-line of the definiteness of children's performance (Car–Boat story, imitations with expansions versus stories); how they may result in the occurrence or non-occurrence of egocentric errors in a given group (three-year-olds' performance in stories versus their performance in games; parental performance in the Cave story versus performance in the procedures discussed in this chapter). Such results may serve as a caution against believing that the competencies we study are uniformly defined homogeneously expressed entities, such that all sorts of operations are equally good for assessing the same competence. Rather we may find that competencies which can be expressed by elegant rules, and apparently should be equally well tested by a number of procedures, may in both children and adults break up along unexpected lines. Through caution in our design and interpretation of experiments — and though comparing our experimental results where possible to naturalistic evidence as well — the regularities may still be found, and the more abstract problems that interest us may yet be analyzed and brought to test. But the complexities of the investigatory process and the competencies we study will no doubt continue to make themselves known, as they have in the investigation of even so apparently modest a domain as the child's acquisition of the English articles.

APPENDIX I

Distribution of comprehension tests (chapter 4)

There were three comprehension periods and three comprehension stories, so each child received one such story at each comprehension period. There were four tests in all for full NPs (article plus noun). Each child received two definites and two indefinites. There was also one pronoun test (*He* or *One*) for each child. See table I.1 for a complete

Table I.1. *Distribution of comprehension tests (chapter 4)*

	Period I		Period II		Period III	
Child	*Task*	*Test*	*Task*	*Test*	*Task*	*Test*
1	Table	TA	Cars	HT	Rabbits	A
2	Table	AT	Cars	OA	Rabbits	T
3	Cars	HT	Table	AT	Rabbits	A
4	Rabbits	T	Cars	OA	Table	AT
5	Cars	HA	Table	TA	Rabbits	T
6	Cars	HA	Rabbits	T	Table	TA
7	Rabbits	A	Table	AT	Cars	OT
8	Cars	OT	Rabbits	A	Table	AT
9	Table	AT	Rabbits	T	Cars	OA
10	Rabbits	T	Cars	HA	Table	AT
11	Cars	OT	Rabbits	A	Table	TA
12	Table	TA	Rabbits	T	Cars	HA
13	Rabbits	A	Table	TA	Cars	HT
14	Cars	OT	Table	TA	Rabbits	A
15	Cars	HA	Table	TA	Rabbits	T
16	Rabbits	A	Cars	HT	Table	TA
17	Table	TA	Rabbits	A	Cars	HT
18	Rabbits	T	Table	AT	Cars	OA
19	Table	AT	Rabbits	T	Cars	OA
20	Rabbits	A	Cars	OT	Table	AT

T = *The X*   H = *He*
A = *A X*   O = *One*

listing. Note that for each child, the two tests of the Table story always disagreed in definiteness. If test 1 was *A X*, then test 2 was *The X*, and vice versa.

A distribution was made up for twenty children and repeated for each age group. The essentials of this design were that every story occurred equally often within each period. Within each story period cell, each test condition also occurred equally often. Tables i.2 and i.3 summarize the distribution of stories and tests within periods. This design, then, fits twenty children within the specifications of tests given to each child.

Table I.2. *Distribution of test conditions and comprehension stories within periods*

	Condition		Story		
	The X	A X	Dogs and Cars	Table	Rabbits
Period I	N=13	N=13	N=7	N=6	N=7
Period II	N=14	N=13	N=6	N=7	N=7
Period III	N=13	N=14	N=7	N=7	N=6
	N=40	N=40	N=20	N=20	N=20

Table I.3. *Distribution of comprehension test conditions within cells defined by story and period*

Period	Dogs and Cars Test 1		Dogs and Cars Test 2		Table Test 1		Table Test 2		Rabbits Test 1	
	He	*One*	*The X*	*A X*	*The X*	*A X*	*The X*	*A X*	*The X*	*A X*
I	N=4	N=3	N=4	N=3	N=3	N=3	N=3	N=3	N=3	N=4
II	N=3	N=3	N=3	N=3	N=4	N=3	N=3	N=4	N=4	N=3
III	N=3	N=4	N=3	N=4	N=3	N=4	N=4	N=3	N=3	N=3
Total	N=10	N=10	N=10	N=10	N=10	N=10	N=10	N=10	N=10	N=10

APPENDIX II

Scores for comprehension tests (chapter 4)

Child	No.	Cars		Table		Rabbits	
3-year-olds		*The X*	*A X*	*The X*	*A X*	*The X*	*A X*
Males	2		R	R	R	R	
	3	R		R	R		R
	6		R	R	W	R	
	7	R		R	R		W
	9		R	R	R	W	
	11	R		R	R		R
	13	R		R	W		W
	16	R		R	W		W
	18		R	R	R	R	
	19		R	R	R	R	
Females	1	R		R	R		W
	4		R	R	R	R	
	5		R	R	R	R	
	8	R		R	R		R

Child	No.	Cars		Table		Rabbits	
	10		R	R	R	R	
	12		W	R	R	W	
	14	R		R	R		R
	15		R	R	R	R	
	17	R		R	R		R
	20	R		R	R		W
4-year-olds							
Males	1	R		R	W		W
	2		W	R	R	W	
	5		R	R	R	W	
	10		R	R	R	R	
	11	R		R	R		W
	12		R	R	R	R	
	13	R		R	R		R
	15		R	R	R	R	
	16	R		R	R		R
	17	R		R	W		R
Females	3	R		R	R		R
	4		R	R	R	R	
	6		W	R	R	R	
	7	R		R	R		W
	8	R		R	R		R

Child	No.	Cars		Table		Rabbits	
	9		R	R	R	R	
	14	R		W	W		R
	18		R	R	W	R	
	19		R	R	R	R	
	20	R		R	W		R

R = Right answer.
W = Wrong answer.

#				
	Out to Meet/I			
8	Like/I Looking For/D Make a Noise/I	Cave/I Toy/D Give/I	Ø → a X/I Hammer–Saw/which Pond/D Knock Over/I Barking/D	Car–Boat/what Out to Meet/D Ø → a X/I
9	Hammer–Saw/which Pond/I Barking/D	Looking For/D Make a Noise/I Car–Boat/what	Toy/I Cave/I Out to Meet/D Give/I	Like/D Knock Over/D Ø → a X/I
10	Toy/I Make a Noise/D Ø → a X/I	Like/D Knock Over/I Cave/D	Hammer–Saw/which Pond/D Out to Meet/I Give/I	Barking/D Looking For/D Car–Boat/what
11	Like/D Give/D Ø → a X/I	Make a Noise/D Looking For/I Car–Boat/which one	Toy/I Barking/D Cave/I Out to Meet/I Give/I	Hammer–Saw/what Pond/I Knock Over/I
12	Looking For/I Car–Boat/what Ø → a X/I	Like/I Cave/I Out to Meet/I	Toy/D Barking/D Make a Noise/D Give/D Like/I	Hammer–Saw/which Pond/D Knock Over/I
13	Hammer–Saw/which	Toy/D	Hammer–Saw/which	Barking/D

APPENDIX III

Distribution of story tests (chapter 5)

The actual design as carried out included a total of thirteen stories: eight systematic stories, and five miscellaneous stories, four of which are described in the main body of the text. The fifth of these was Hammer–Saw. This story, like Car–Boat, was designed to test the effect of question-phrase on answering. The story is given below:

13. Hammer–Saw. $a\,X \to a\,X$

    A child is building a wooden box, and decides he needs a hammer and a saw. He asks his father for both. His father says that buying both would be too expensive, and that the child can have just one. The child says he wants both, and the father says only one. Finally, his father gives him enough money to buy just one, and the child goes to the store. Definite question form: 'Which did he buy?' Indefinite question form: 'What did he buy?'

The basis for the story is that occasionally adults will so build up a representation of a possibility that it seems to acquire specificity of its own. People say things such as 'If I were you I'd buy the hammer, not the saw', even though they are not talking about particular objects but choices. So the answer seemed shiftable in terms of the question phrase. (The results from the four-year-olds, the only group to receive Hammer–Saw, shows a shift in definiteness according to question word similar to that found in Car–Boat. Four of five answers obtained by *which* were definite, and just three of nine obtained by *what* were definite expressions.)

In the original design, each child of both age groups was to receive all thirteen stories. Later Toy and Hammer–Saw were dropped from the three-year-olds (see discussion above, p. 50). Thirteen stories divided by four periods does not come out even. After pilot work it seemed to me that children were most receptive of the stories in the third period, at the beginning of the second experimental session. Accordingly, the odd story was placed in the third period for all children. Thus each child received three stories in each of periods I, II, and IV, and four stories in period III. A complete listing of the stories assigned to each subject is given in table III.1. This comprises the design carried out in testing. I did occasionally give the wrong version of a story through forgetfulness. This, however, was quite rare.

Stories were distributed proportionately over the four periods, so that as far as was possible, each story appeared equally often in each period. Of the stories which appeared in two versions, each version appeared equally often within each period, again insofar as was possible. In table III.2 the frequency with which each story was asked of children in each period is given. These numbers apply to the twenty-subject design done for each age group. Below I give the number of definite and indefinite versions presented in each period just for the eight systematic stories. D = 18, for example, means that a definite-eliciting story was asked eighteen times.

Period II	Period III	Period IV
D = 18	D = 19	D = 25	D = 18
I = 18	I = 19	I = 24	I = 19

Table III.3 lists the distribution of stories and conditions for the eight systematic stories in fuller detail, giving the number of times the definite and indefinite versions were asked for each story in each period. For all stories, $D = A\ X \rightarrow The\ X$. For the first five stories (*Out to Meet* through *Give*), $I = X's \rightarrow A\ X$. For the last three stories, $I = A\ X \rightarrow A\ X$.

The two stories testing for the effect of question word, Hammer—Saw and Car—Boat, also appeared each in two versions. Their distribution is given in table III.4; in this table, D = definite question word, i.e. *which one* for Car—Boat and *which* for Hammer—Saw; I = indefinite question word, i.e. *what*.

Within the limits described in the last pages, assignment of story and condition to child and period was random.

Table III.1. *Distribution of stories tests (chapter 5)*

Child No.	Period I	Period II	Period III	Period IV
1	Looking For/D Cave/I Give/I	Like/I Make a Noise/D $\emptyset \rightarrow a\ X$/I	Hammer—Saw/*what* Pond/D Knock Over/I Car—Boat/*which one*	Toy/D Barking/D Out to Meet/I Looking For/I
2	Toy/I Barking/D Give/I	Hammer—Saw/*which* Pond/D Knock Over/I	Like/D Car—Boat/*which*	

Table III.1. *(continued)*

Child No.	Period I	Period II	Period III	Period IV
7	Like/I Knock Over/D	Barking/D Looking For/D	Hammer—Saw/*what* Pond/I Cave/I	Toy/D Make a Noise/D Give/I

	Cave/I Out to Meet/I	Knock Over/I Pond/D	Looking For/D Car–Boat/*what* ∅ → *a* X/I	Make a Noise/D Give/I
14	Hammer–Saw/*which* Pond/D Knock Over/I	Looking For/I Car–Boat/*what* Out to Meet/D	Toy/D Barking/D Cave/I Give/D	Like/I Make a Noise/I ∅ → *a* X/I
15	Make a Noise/I Car–Boat/*which one* Out to Meet/D	Like/D Knock Over/D ∅ → *a* X/I	Hammer–Saw/*what* Pond/I Looking For/D Cave/I	Toy/I Barking/D Give/I
16	Looking For/I Car–Boat/*what* ∅ → *a* X/I	Hammer–Saw/*which* Pond/I Give/D	Like/D Knock Over/D Make a Noise/D Out to Meet/I	Toy/I Cave/I Barking/D
17	Like/D Knock Over/D Make a Noise/D	Barking/D Out to Meet/I Give/I	Toy/I Looking For/D Car–Boat/*which one* ∅ → *a* X/I	Hammer–Saw/*what* Pond/I Cave/I
18	Toy/D Barking/D Cave/I	Hammer–Saw/*what* Pond/I Knock Over/D	Like/I Make a Noise/I Give/D ∅ → *a* X/I	Looking For/I Car–Boat/*which one* Out to Meet/D
19	Cave/I	Like/D	Hammer–Saw/*which*	Toy/I

Table III.1. (*continued*)

Child No.	Period I	Period II	Period III	Period IV
	Out to Meet/D	Looking For/I	Pond/I	Give/D
	Car–Boat/*what*	Make a Noise/I	Knock Over/D	$\emptyset \rightarrow a\ X$/I
			Barking/D	
20	Hammer–Saw/*what*	Toy/I	Like/D	Make a Noise/D
	Pond/D	Barking/D	Knock Over/I	Cave/I
	Give/D	$\emptyset \rightarrow a\ X$/I	Looking For/I	Out to Meet/I
			Car–Boat/*which one*	

D = *The X* is correct answer.
I = *A X* is correct answer.

Table III.2. *Distribution of the stories across story periods*

Story	Period I	Period II	Period III	Period IV
Out to Meet	N=4	N=5	N=6	N=5
Make a Noise	N=4	N=5	N=6	N=5
Pond	N=5	N=5	N=6	N=4
Knock Over	N=5	N=5	N=6	N=4
Give	N=4	N=4	N=7	N=5
Like	N=5	N=5	N=6	N=4
Looking For	N=4	N=5	N=6	N=5
Toy	N=5	N=4	N=6	N=5
Car—Boat	N=4	N=5	N=7	N=4
Hammer—Saw	N=5	N=5	N=6	N=4
Barking	N=5	N=4	N=6	N=5
$\emptyset \rightarrow a\,X$	N=5	N=4	N=6	N=5
Cave	N=5	N=4	N=6	N=5
	N=60	N=60	N=80	N=60

Table III.3. *Distribution of stories and versions for the systematic stories*

Story	Period I	Period II	Period III	Period IV
Out to Meet	D=2	D=3	D=3	D=2
	I=2	I=3	I=2	I=3
Make a Noise	D=2	D=2	D=3	D=3
	I=2	I=3	I=3	I=2
Pond	D=2	D=3	D=3	D=2
	I=3	I=2	I=3	I=2
Knock Over	D=3	D=2	D=3	D=2
	I=2	I=3	I=3	I=2
Give	D=2	D=2	D=4	D=2
	I=2	I=3	I=3	I=2
Like	D=2	D=3	D=3	D=2
	I=3	I=2	I=3	I=2
Looking For	D=2	D=2	D=3	D=3
	I=2	I=3	I=3	I=2
Toy	D=3	D=2	D=3	D=2
	I=2	I=2	I=3	I=3
	D=18	D=19	D=25	D=18
	I=18	I=19	I=24	I=19

Table III.4. *Distribution of definite and indefinite versions for Q-word stories*

Story	Period I	Period II	Period III	Period IV
Car—Boat	D=2	D=2	D=4	D=2
	I=2	I=3	I=3	I=2
Hammer—Saw	D=3	D=2	D=3	D=2
	I=2	I=3	I=3	I=2
	D=5	D=4	D=7	D=4
	I=4	I=6	I=6	I=4

APPENDIX IV

Distribution of scores for stories (chapter 6)

Child	No.	Out to Meet T	A	Make a Noise T	A	Pond T	A	Knock Over T	A	Give T	A	Looking For T	A	Toy T	A	Like T	A
3-year-olds																	
Males	2										a						
	3	t				aa			a								
	6	t			a			t		t							
	7		t	a		a		t			a	a					a
	9	t									a					t	
	11		t	t			t	t		t			a			t	
	13		a	a		a			a		a	t					a
	16		t	t			a	t		a			t			a	
	18	a			a		a	a		t			a				a
		a			a		a	a		t			a				a
Females	1		a	t		a			a		a	t					a
	4		a	t			a	a		t			a			t	
	5	t			a	a			t		a	t					a
	8	a			t	a			a		a	t					a
	10			t					a		a					t	
	12		a	t		a			a	a			a				t
	14	tt			t	tt			a	a			t				a
	15	tt					a	t			a	t				t	
	17					a		t			a	t				t	
	20			t		a			a	a			a			a	
4-year-olds																	
Males	1			t						t		t					a
	2	t			t	a			a		a	t			a	t	
	5	t			a				a		a			t			a
	10		t	t		t			a	t		a			ɑ	t	
	11	t		**a**						t			a		t	t	
	12		a	t		t		ta		t			a	t			a
	13		t	t		t			a	t		t		t			a
	15	t			a		a	t			a	t			a	t	

Child	No.	Out to Meet T	Out to Meet A	Make a Noise T	Make a Noise A	Pond T	Pond A	Knock Over T	Knock Over A	Give T	Give A	Looking For T	Looking For A	Toy T	Toy A	Like T	Like A
	16												a				
	17		t	t			t	t			a	t			a	t	
Females	3	t			a	t			a	t			a	t				t
	4		a	t			a	t		t			a		t	t		
	6	t			a		a	t		t			a	a				a
	7		a	t			a	t			a	t		t				
	8	t			a	t			a		a	t		a				a
	9	t			a		t	t			a	t			t	t		
	14	t			t	t			t	t			a	t				t
	18	t			a		a	t		t			a	t				t
	19	t			a		a	t		t			a					a
	20		a	t		a			a	t			a		a	t		

Child	No.	Car–Boat which one	Car–Boat what	Hammer–Saw which	Hammer–Saw what	Cave A	Barking T	∅ → a X subject	∅ → a X object
3-year-olds									
Males	2								
	3						tt		
	6		a			a	a		a
	7	a				a	a	a	a
	9					t		t	a
	11	t				a	t	a	
	13		a				a	a	
	16	t				a	t	a	
	18	a					aa	a	
	19		a			a	a	a	
Females	1	a					t	a	
	4		a						a
	5		a			t	t	a	a
	8	a				t	t	a	
	10					a		a	
	12		a			a	a		a
	14		a			t	t	a	aa
	15	t				a	t	a	
	17	t				t	t	a	
	20	a				t	at		a
4-year-olds									
Males	1					t	t		a
	2	t			a	t	t	a	
	5		a			a	t		aa
	10		t	a		t	t	a	
	11					a	t		a
	12		a	t		a	t	a	

Child	No.	Car–Boat which one	what	Hammer–Saw which	what	Cave A	Barking T	∅ → a X subject	object
	13		a	t		t	t	t	
	15	t			a	a	t	a	
	16					t			a
	17	t			t	t	t		a
Females	3		t	tt		a	t		aa
	4	t			t	a	t	a	
	6		a		a	a	t	a	
	7	t			a	t	a	t	
	8	a			a	a	t		a
	9	t				a	t	a	
	14		t	t		t	t	t	
	18	t			t	t*	t	a	
	19		t			a	t	a	
	20	t			a	a	t	a	

T = *The X* is the correct answer.
A = *A X* is the correct answer.
t = Definite answer given.
a = Indefinite answer given.
*Correct definite expression: subject replied 'the biggest girl'.

APPENDIX V

Method of scoring imitations

Scoring proceeded in two steps, starting with a score of 1.00 for each sentence for each child:

(1) The proportion of words the child did not imitate was subtracted. E.g., if a child did not render three words of an eight-word sentence, 0.38 was subtracted.

(2) 0.25 was subtracted (at most once) if a child also failed to imitate or distorted a structurally significant part of the sentence.

Example: Subject 13 of the three-year-olds, sentence 12
Sentence: THE BOY WHO THE MAN SAW STARTED TO LAUGH.
Imitation: The boy Ø Ø Ø Ø started to laugh.

(1) Four words out of nine were not imitated, resulting in a subtraction of 0.44 (4/9).

(2) A major structural mistake was made, the deletion of a relative clause, resulting in the subtraction of 0.25
Final score: $1.00 - 0.44 - 0.25 = 0.31$.

APPENDIX VI

Imitations (chapter 6)

1. I am very tall.
2. It goes in a big box.
3. Two of the marbles rolled away.
4. I saw a table and a red chair.
5. A girl got hit by a fast car.
6. He ate some ice cream because he wanted to.
7. I saw a boy who was wearing a blue coat.
8. I don't know why those people aren't sitting down.
9. I'm over here and you're over there.
10. The girl who jumped over the fence fell down.
11. I like to ride in cars.
12. The boy who the man saw started to laugh.
13. I think I hear a cat meowing.
14. What I would like is to build a big house.

Imitation scores for each child (chapter 6)

Child	No.	Sentence 1	2	3	4	5	6	7
3-year-olds								
Males	2	1	1	1	1	0	1	1
	3	1	0.08	0.08	0.50	0.37	0.52	0.08
	6	0	0	1	0.08	1	0.30	0.45
	7	1	1	0.67	0.75	0.88	0.30	0
	9	1	0.83	0.83	0.46	0.25	0.44	0.25
	11	1	1	0	1	0.88	1	0.90
	13	0.75	0.67	0.25	0.89	0.88	0.67	1
	16	0.75	0.83	0.25	0.50	0.13	0.63	0.05
	18	1	1	0.08	1	1	1	0.55
	19	0.75	0.67	0.57	0.86	0.50	0	0.25
Females	1	1	1	0.67	0.88	1	0.38	1
	4	1	0.67	0	0	0	0.17	0.25
	5	1	0.83	0.25	0.65	0.75	1	0.55
	8	0.75	0.58	0	0.75	0.88	0.67	0.45
	10	1	1	0.67	1	1	0.89	0.45
	12	—	—	—	—	—	—	—
	14	—	—	—	—	—	—	—
	15	1	1	1	1	1	0.89	0.65
	17	1	0.83	1	0.89	0	0.44	0.45
	20	1	1	0.83	1	0.88	1	0.90
4-year-olds								
Males	1	1	1	0.42	0.88	1	0.89	0.45
	2	1	0.83	1	1	0.88	1	1
	5	1	1	0.83	1	1	1	1
	10	1	0.42	0.83	0.50	1	1	0.55
	11	1	0.83	1	1	0.75	1	1
	12	1	1	1	1	1	1	0.90
	13	1	1	0.86	1	1	1	1
	15	1	1	1	1	1	1	1
	16	1	1	0.83	1	1	0.52	0.45
	17	0.75	1	1	1	0.89	1	1
Females	3	1	1	1	1	1	1	1
	4	1	1	1	1	1	1	1
	6	1	1	1	1	1	1	0.90
	7	0.75	1	0.25	0.50	0.88	0.89	0.45
	8	1	1	1	1	1	1	1
	9	1	1	1	1	0.88	1	0.90
	14	1	0.83	1	1	1	1	0.90
	18	1	0.83	1	1	1	1	0.90
	19	1	1	1	1	1	1	1
	20	1	1	1	1	1	1	0.90

APPENDIX III

Distribution of story tests (chapter 5)

The actual design as carried out included a total of thirteen stories: eight systematic stories, and five miscellaneous stories, four of which are described in the main body of the text. The fifth of these was Hammer–Saw. This story, like Car–Boat, was designed to test the effect of question-phrase on answering. The story is given below:

13. Hammer–Saw. $a\,X \rightarrow a\,X$

    A child is building a wooden box, and decides he needs a hammer and a saw. He asks his father for both. His father says that buying both would be too expensive, and that the child can have just one. The child says he wants both, and the father says only one. Finally, his father gives him enough money to buy just one, and the child goes to the store. Definite question form: *'Which* did he buy?' Indefinite question form: *'What* did he buy?'

The basis for the story is that occasionally adults will so build up a representation of a possibility that it seems to acquire specificity of its own. People say things such as 'If I were you I'd buy the hammer, not the saw', even though they are not talking about particular objects but choices. So the answer seemed shiftable in terms of the question phrase. (The results from the four-year-olds, the only group to receive Hammer–Saw, shows a shift in definiteness according to question word similar to that found in Car–Boat. Four of five answers obtained by *which* were definite, and just three of nine obtained by *what* were definite expressions.)

In the original design, each child of both age groups was to receive all thirteen stories. Later Toy and Hammer–Saw were dropped from the three-year-olds (see discussion above, p. 50). Thirteen stories divided by four periods does not come out even. After pilot work it seemed to me that children were most receptive of the stories in the third period, at the beginning of the second experimental session. Accordingly, the odd story was placed in the third period for all children. Thus each child received three stories in each of periods I, II, and IV, and four stories in period III. A complete listing of the stories assigned to each subject is given in table III.1. This comprises the design carried out in testing. I did occasionally give the wrong version of a story through forgetfulness. This, however, was quite rare.

Stories were distributed proportionately over the four periods, so that as far as was possible, each story appeared equally often in each period. Of the stories which appeared in two versions, each version appeared equally often within each period, again insofar as was possible. In table III.2 the frequency with which each story was asked of children in each period is given. These numbers apply to the twenty-subject design done for each age group. Below I give the number of definite and indefinite versions presented in each period just for the eight systematic stories. D = 18, for example, means that a definite-eliciting story was asked eighteen times.

	Period II	Period III	Period IV
D=18	D=19	D=25	D=18
I=18	I=19	I=24	I=19

Table III.3 lists the distribution of stories and conditions for the eight systematic stories in fuller detail, giving the number of times the definite and indefinite versions were asked for each story in each period. For all stories, $D = A\ X \rightarrow The\ X$. For the first five stories (*Out to Meet* through *Give*), $I = X's \rightarrow A\ X$. For the last three stories, $I = A\ X \rightarrow A\ X$.

The two stories testing for the effect of question word, Hammer—Saw and Car—Boat, also appeared each in two versions. Their distribution is given in table III.4; in this table, D = definite question word, i.e. *which one* for Car—Boat and *which* for Hammer—Saw; I = indefinite question word, i.e. *what*.

Within the limits described in the last pages, assignment of story and condition to child and period was random.

Table III.1. *Distribution of stories tests (chapter 5)*

Child No.	Period I	Period II	Period III	Period IV
1	Looking For/D Cave/I Give/I	Like/I Make a Noise/D $\emptyset \to a\ X$/I	Hammer–Saw/*what* Pond/D Knock Over/I Car–Boat/*which one*	Toy/D Barking/D Out to Meet/I
2	Toy/I Barking/D Give/I	Hammer–Saw/*which* Pond/D Knock Over/I	Like/D Car–Boat/*which one* Out to Meet/D $\emptyset \to a\ X$/I	Looking For/D Make a Noise/I Cave/I
3	Cave/I Toy/D Barking/D	Hammer–Saw/*which* Pond/D Out to Meet/D	Looking For/I Make a Noise/I Car–Boat/*what* Give/D	Like/I Knock Over/I $\emptyset \to a\ X$/I
4	Hammer–Saw/*what* Pond/I Knock Over/D	Cave/I Toy/I Give/D	Barking/D Looking For/I Make a Noise/D $\emptyset \to a\ X$/I	Like/D Out to Meet/I Car–Boat/*what*
5	Like/I Knock Over/I $\emptyset \to a\ X$/I	Barking/D Out to Meet/D Car–Boat/*what*	Toy/D Make a Noise/I Cave/I Give/I	Hammer–Saw/*which* Pond/D Looking For/D
6	Hammer–Saw/*which* Pond/I Barking/D	Toy/D Make a Noise/I $\emptyset \to a\ X$/I	Like/I Knock Over/D Out to Meet/D Car–Boat/*what*	Looking For/I Cave/I Give/D

Table III.1. (*continued*)

Child No.	Period I	Period II	Period III	Period IV
7	Like/I Knock Over/D Out to Meet/I	Barking/D Looking For/D Car–Boat/*which one*	Hammer–Saw/*what* Pond/I Cave/I $\emptyset \to a\ X$/I	Toy/D Make a Noise/D Give/I
8	Like/I Looking For/D Make a Noise/I	Cave/I Toy/D Give/I	Hammer–Saw/*which* Pond/D Knock Over/I Barking/D	Car–Boat/*what* Out to Meet/D $\emptyset \to a\ X$/I
9	Hammer–Saw/*which* Pond/I Barking/D	Looking For/D Make a Noise/I Car–Boat/*what*	Toy/I Cave/I Out to Meet/D Give/I	Like/D Knock Over/D $\emptyset \to a\ X$/I
10	Toy/I Make a Noise/D $\emptyset \to a\ X$/I	Like/D Knock Over/I Cave/D	Hammer–Saw/*which* Pond/D Out to Meet/I Give/I	Barking/D Looking For/D Car–Boat/*what*
11	Like/D Give/D $\emptyset \to a\ X$/I	Make a Noise/D Looking For/I Car–Boat/*which one*	Toy/I Barking/D Cave/I Out to Meet/I	Hammer–Saw/*what* Pond/I Knock Over/D
12	Looking For/I Car–Boat/*what* $\emptyset \to a\ X$/I	Like/I Cave/I Out to Meet/I	Toy/D Barking/D Make a Noise/D Give/D	Hammer–Saw/*which* Pond/D Knock Over/I
13	Toy/D	Hammer–Saw/*which*	Like/I	Barking/D

8	9	10	11	12	13	14
1	1	0.63	1	1	1	1
0.30	0.75	0.30	1	0.30	0.23	0.45
0.77	0.17	0	1	0	0.33	0
0.30	0	0.52	0.42	0	0.17	0.35
0.77	0.90	0.52	0.83	0.30	0.71	0.45
1	1	1	1	0.52	1	0
0.77	0.75	0.30	1	0.30	0.77	0
0.67	0.75	0.30	1	0.08	0.86	0.05
0.88	0.75	0.55	0.67	0.42	0.86	0.05
0	0.86	0	1	0.08	0	0.05
0.45	0.77	0.52	1	0.52	0.71	0.45
0	0.46	0.30	0.42	0	0	0
0.89	1	0.63	0	0.52	1	0.45
0.77	0.86	0.42	0.50	0.08	0.46	0.45
0.77	0.75	0.52	1	0.52	0	0.05
—	—	—	—	—	—	—
—	—	—	—	—	—	—
0.89	1	0.63	1	0.30	0	0.45
0.89	0.75	0.63	0.83	0.19	0	0.15
0.89	0.61	0.75	1	1	0.61	0.90
0.08	1	0.89	1	0.70	0.56	0.45
0.89	0.75	0.52	1	0.89	0.71	0.80
1	1	1	1	1	1	0.90
0.77	0.61	0.42	1	0.63	0.86	0.55
1	1	1	1	1	0.86	1
1	1	1	1	1	1	0.90
1	1	0.64	1	0.64	0.86	0.55
1	1	1	1	1	1	0.90
0.89	0.61	0.42	1	0.30	0.45	0.55
0.89	1	1	1	0.89	0.86	0.65
1	1	1	1	1	1	1
1	1	1	1	1	0.86	0.25
0.89	0.75	1	1	1	1	0.90
0.89	1	0.42	1	0.42	0.86	0.35
1	1	1	1	1	1	0.90
1	1	0.30	1	0.64	1	0.90
0.89	0.61	0.90	1	0.79	0.86	0.90
1	1	0.89	1	1	0.86	1
1	1	1	1	1	1	1
1	1	0.89	1	1	0.86	1

APPENDIX VIII

Scores for imitations with expansions

Child	No.	Monkey T	Monkey A	Pencil T	Pencil A
3-year-olds					
Males	2	t			a
	3	t			a
	6		—	t	
	7		a	t	
	9	t			a
	11		—	t	
	13	t			—
	16	t			a
	18	—			a
	19		a	t	
Females	1		—	t	
	4	—			a
	5		a	—	
	8	—			a
	14		t	t	
	15	t			t
	17		a	—	
	20	t			—

T = *The X* is the correct answer.
A = *A X* is the correct answer.
t = Definite answer given.
a = Indefinite answer given.
— = No article given or non-article form given.
Monkey story always given first.

APPENDIX IX

Distribution of game tests (chapter 8)

There were four testing periods, two each per experimental session. A child played each game twice, once each session. One game was played each testing period (see above p. 83 for additional general details). A complete listing of which game was played in which number condition is given in table IX.1.

Table IX.1. *Distribution of tests for games (chapter 8)*

	Period I		Period II		Period III		Period IV	
Child	*Game*	*Cond.*	*Game*	*Cond.*	*Game*	*Cond.*	*Game*	*Cond.*
1	Dragon	A	Hill	T	Dragon	T	Hill	A
2	Hill	A	Dragon	T	Dragon	A	Hill	T
3	Dragon	A	Hill	T	Dragon	T	Hill	A
4	Dragon	T	Hill	A	Dragon	A	Hill	T
5	Hill	T	Dragon	A	Dragon	T	Hill	A
6	Dragon	A	Hill	T	Hill	A	Dragon	T
7	Hill	A	Dragon	T	Hill	T	Dragon	A
8	Hill	T	Dragon	A	Hill	A	Dragon	T
9	Dragon	T	Hill	A	Hill	T	Dragon	A
10	Dragon	A	Hill	T	Dragon	T	Hill	A
11	Dragon	T	Hill	A	Hill	T	Dragon	A
12	Hill	A	Dragon	T	Dragon	A	Hill	T
13	Dragon	T	Hill	A	Hill	T	Dragon	A
14	Hill	A	Dragon	T	Dragon	A	Hill	T
15	Hill	T	Dragon	A	Hill	A	Dragon	T
16	Dragon	T	Hill	A	Hill	T	Dragon	A
17	Hill	T	Dragon	A	Dragon	T	Hill	A
18	Hill	A	Dragon	T	Hill	T	Dragon	A
19	Hill	T	Dragon	A	Hill	A	Dragon	T
20	Dragon	A	Hill	T	Dragon	T	Hill	A

T = *The X* is the correct answer.
A = *A X* is the correct answer.

Distribution of the tests across periods and subjects

As with the other procedures, a single design was constructed for twenty subjects and then repeated for each age group. Across twenty subjects each game was played the times in each period. Each number condition was given equally often in each period. Within a given game-period cell each number condition was again evenly distributed. Tables ix.2, ix.3 and ix.4 illustrate these distributions, first for games alone, then number conditions, and then both together. Within these limits, and those prescribed by what each child was to receive, assignment of condition to each child was random.

Table IX.2. *Distribution of games across periods*

	Dragon	Down the Hill
Period I	N = 10	N = 10
Period II	N = 10	N = 10
Period III	N = 10	N = 10
Period IV	N = 10	N = 10

Table IX.3. *Distribution of number conditions across periods*

	Singular	Plural
Period I	N = 10	N = 10
Period II	N = 10	N = 10
Period III	N = 10	N = 10
Period IV	N = 10	N = 10

Table IX.4. *Distribution of game and number conditions across periods*

| | Singular | | Plural | |
	Dragon	Down the Hill	Dragon	Down the Hill
Period I	N = 5	N = 5	N = 5	N = 5
Period II	N = 5	N = 5	N = 5	N = 5
Period III	N = 5	N = 5	N = 5	N = 5
Period IV	N = 5	N = 5	N = 5	N = 5

APPENDIX X

Distribution of scores for games (chapter 8)

Child	No.	Down the Hill				Dragon			
		T (singular)		A (plural)		T (singular)		A (plural)	
		V	I	V	I	V	I	V	I
3-year-olds		V	I	V	I	V	I	V	I
Males	2	—	—	1.00	1.00	1.00	0.50	—	—
	3	1.00	1.00	—	—	—	—	1.00	1.00
	6	1.00	0.50	1.00	1.00	0.00	0.50	1.00	1.00
	7	0.50	1.00	0.00	1.00	—	—	1.00	1.00
	9	1.00	1.00	1.00	0.50	1.00	1.00	0.00	0.50
	11	1.00	1.00	0.00	1.00	1.00	0.00	0.00	0.50
	13	0.50	0.50	0.00	1.00	1.00	—	—	1.00
	16	0.00	0.00	1.00	1.00	1.00	1.00	1.00	1.00
	18	0.50	1.00	1.00	1.00	0.50	0.00	1.00	1.00
	19	0.00	0.50	1.00	1.00	0.50	0.00	0.00	0.75
Females	1	1.00	1.00	0.00	0.50	0.50	0.50	1.00	1.00
	4	1.00	1.00	1.00	0.50	1.00	0.50	1.00	1.00
	5	1.00	0.50	0.00	1.00	1.00	1.00	1.00	1.00
	8	1.00	1.00	0.50	1.00	0.00	0.00	1.00	1.00
	10	1.00	1.00	1.00	1.00	1.00	0.50	1.00	1.00
	12	0.00	0.00	0.50	1.00	1.00	0.00	1.00	1.00
	14	1.00	1.00	1.00	1.00	1.00	—	1.00	1.00
	15	1.00	1.00	0.50	1.00	1.00	0.00	0.00	1.00
	17	1.00	1.00	0.00	0.50	1.00	0.00	1.00	1.00
	20	1.00	0.50	0.50	1.00	0.00	0.00	1.00	1.00
4-year-olds									
Males	1	1.00	1.00	—	—	—	—	0.00	1.00
	2	0.50	1.00	1.00	1.00	0.00	0.00	1.00	1.00
	5	1.00	1.00	1.00	1.00	1.00	1.00	1.00	1.00
	10	1.00	1.00	0.00	0.50	0.00	1.00	0.50	1.00
	11	1.00	1.00	0.50	1.00	0.00	—	0.50	1.00

Child	No.	Down the Hill				Dragon			
		T (singular)		A (plural)		T (singular)		A (plural)	
	12	1.00	0.50	0.00	0.50	1.00	0.00	0.50	1.00
	13	1.00	1.00	1.00	1.00	1.00	1.00	0.00	0.50
	15	1.00	1.00	—	1.00	1.00	1.00	1.00	1.00
	16	1.00	1.00	0.00	1.00	0.50	0.50	1.00	1.00
	17	1.00	1.00	0.00	—	1.00	1.00	1.00	1.00
Females	3	1.00	1.00	1.00	1.00	1.00	1.00	1.00	1.00
	4	1.00	1.00	1.00	1.00	1.00	1.00	1.00	1.00
	6	1.00	1.00	1.00	1.00	1.00	1.00	1.00	1.00
	7	1.00	1.00	1.00	—	1.00	—	1.00	1.00
	8	1.00	0.00	1.00	1.00	1.00	1.00	1.00	1.00
	9	1.00	1.00	1.00	1.00	1.00	1.00	1.00	0.50
	14	1.00	1.00	1.00	1.00	1.00	1.00	0.00	0.00
	18	1.00	1.00	1.00	1.00	1.00	1.00	1.00	1.00
	19	1.00	1.00	—	—	—	—	1.00	1.00
	20	1.00	1.00	1.00	—	1.00	1.00	0.50	0.50

T = Definite-eliciting condition.
A = Indefinite-eliciting condition.
V = Toys visible.
I = Toys invisible.

APPENDIX XI

A few problems in the semantics of articles

As noted in the first chapter, a brief discussion of any commonly used set of words of a language invariably fails to include various difficulties, shadings, and exceptions characteristic of the full use of the words. The case with articles is no different. I have attempted to point out some of these problems or exceptions in the present appendix, in varying degrees of detail

Colloquial use of this

Because of the ambiguity of indefinite articles as being either completely non-specific in reference, or specific for the speaker but not the listener, some indefinite expressions may be ambiguous. Consider

(1) I'm looking for *a doctor*.

The speaker might mean that there is a particular doctor he is looking for. In that case he might continue 'Can you help me find him? His name is Blaidell, and he is a liver specialist.' On the other hand, he might have no particular doctor in mind himself, as shown by the following continuation 'Can you help me find one? I need one that can treat liver ailments.' In colloquial speech a speaker may often use the definite demonstrative *this* rather than *a* for a reference specific for himself but not his listener. The sentence below

(2) I'm looking for *this house*.

lacks the ambiguity of (1); it implies that the speaker has a particular house in mind. In more normal use *this* is a demonstrative the speaker uses to refer to things physically close to him, as in

133

(3) Come over here and look at *this chair*.

Often it can be used, in fact, when the speaker has something in his own focus of attention which the listener may not. In its speaker-specific, listener-non-specific use, as in (2) above, *this* has properties conceptually similar to its normal use. It does not seem coincidental, for example, that *this* provides this new form rather than *that*, which implies objects relatively far away from the speaker.

A problem with entailment

Karttunen (1968b), to whom the concept of entailment is due, has noticed there is not a straightforward definitional relation between the use of definite articles and the referential context that enables their use. Consider Karttunen's example cited above in chapter 1:

(4) I was driving on the freeway the other day when suddenly *the engine* began to make a funny noise. I stopped *the car* and when I opened *the hood*, I saw that *the radiator* was boiling.

It is the fact that driving entails a car, which in turn entails a particular engine, hood, and radiator, that allows definite reference to be made in the italicized phrases above. But Karttunen points out that not all cars have radiators: Volkswagens do not. Yet a speaker knowing this could still say *the radiator* in the passage above. Accordingly he revised the formulation: one can refer to *the radiator* because many cars do have radiators, and those that do have just one.

This revision does not allow any definite reference to be made. Karttunen cites an example where the entailed existence of the referent is quite doubtful (Karttunen, 1968b, p. 10):

(5) I was driving down the freeway when suddenly *the parachute* opened.

If cars customarily possessed parachutes, (5) might sound more reasonable, but of course they presently do not.

What is at stake, then, is that entailment may only need to be plausible rather than necessary. The instance of *the radiator* may not be completely convincing, because doubtless many people, especially in America, think all cars have radiators. But related examples are easily found. I do not think that (6) would cause difficulties to a listener even if he did not already know that the speaker possessed an air conditioner:

> (6) What a time we had at home last night. *The air-conditioner* broke down.

Many American households have air-conditioners, but certainly not all. Similarly, one could refer to *the dishwasher* without introduction. But consider (7):

> (7) We wanted to take a trip to the country yesterday, but *the helicopter* wasn't working.

A naive listener would probably be surprised, and might even ask 'You have a helicopter?'

Clearly a makeshift repair of the type devised by Karttunen is necessary. As a general linguistic rule, attempting a list of empirical formulations like 'Many houses have air-conditioners' or 'All cars have engines' or 'Few households have helicopters' is obviously clumsy. The real principle appears to be firmly psychological: the speaker should not violate the listener's range of reasonable expectations. When a definite expression is used, it should be easy for the listener to locate the particular referent for it according to previous conversational context or general knowledge. As providing a unique reference becomes more difficult because of the implausibility of the necessary induction, the reference becomes less successful. To refer to *the car* and *the engine* after mentioning driving sets the listener an easy psychological location task. Reference to *the air-conditioner* or *the dishwasher* requires a slightly more difficult retrieval perhaps, but the basic process is still a simple one. The listener, in effect, can fill in 'Oh, he has an air-conditioner at home, many people do. That's the one he means.' But a reference to *the helicopter* assumes that the location is easy for the listener, which it is not. The speaker should overtly introduce such unusual circumstances, saying something like 'We have *a helicopter*, but it wasn't working' — unless he talks with people who commonly have helicopters themselves. In fact, there is a range of courtesy for speakers. It seems mandatory to introduce a helicopter. Before referring to *the air-conditioner*, a very cautious speaker might make an overt introduction by saying 'We have an air-conditioner at home,' since some people do and some do not. But to introduce the engine of a car would be absurd: 'I was driving down the freeway the other day. I was driving my car, and it has an engine, and the engine started to make a funny noise.' Talking like this indicates that the speaker believes the listener to be an idiot, since the information is redundant.

I have discussed related problems with entailment elsewhere (Maratsos, 1971), but that discussion adds nothing substantially different to the facts noted above.

Non-specific reference to particular referents

There are clear instances in which the speaker is speaking about a particular class member, and may be certain his listener would be able to place just the class member he is referring to, and yet makes indefinite reference to it. Such reference seems contradictory to the general principles discussed in chapter 1. I cannot really do more here than describe the phenomenon.

Apparently what the speaker may do is refer to something in its role as no particular member of its class, as simply an example. I give some examples below:

> (8) Someone comes on a friend who generally dislikes children and finds him playing with one. Talking about it afterwards, he says 'Well, it was nice to see you playing with *a child*.'
> (9) Two friends go out hunting, and one of them shoots a duck out of season. The other one says, 'You shouldn't have shot *a duck*, ducks are out of season.'
> (10) One of two roommates takes out a girl from Vassar on a date. His roommate meets the girl before the date. When the first one gets back, his roommate asks, 'Well, how did you like taking out *a girl from Vassar?*'

In all these cases, it seems clear that the speaker only cares about the referent the italic phrase describes in terms of its being a perfectly typical example of its class, not in terms of its particular distinguishing features. The meaning intended becomes intuitively clear when a contrasting definite form is used:

> (10) How did you like taking out *a girl from Vassar*?
> (11) How did you like taking out *the girl from Vassar*?

The definite expression in (11) implies that the speaker is interested in the girl herself — was she interesting, fun, affable, and so on. The question in (10) is about her as just a representative of the general class *girl from Vassar*. The speaker seems to want to know how it would be to take out any girl from Vassar, and this particular one is only a non-distinctive sample. Because of this possibility of making either specific or non-specific reference to a particular class member, statements like 'I dated *a girl from Vassar* last night' can take either of the two above senses for him. The speaker might intend the non-specific sense if he were enumerating what colleges he had been dating girls from: 'Last week I dated *a girl from Radcliffe*, last night I saw *a girl from Vassar*, and tomorrow I'm taking out *a girl from Yale*.' His concern is not with the girl from Vassar as a particular person, but as an example of her class. On the other hand, a speaker intending to talk about her in particular might begin 'I dated a girl from Vassar last night,' and continue 'She was pretty interesting, and I think I'll see her again.' This sense of having the girl in mind as a particular girl (from Vassar) is rendered well in the more colloquial 'I dated *this girl from Vassar* last night.'

Generic definite and indefinite expressions

Generic expressions include the following examples:

(12) Dogs howl at the moon.
(13) A beaver builds dams.
(14) The llama lives in South America.

Generic sentences characterize general properties of classes, rather than being about particular members. Definite or indefinite articles may be used, though it seems that indefinite expressions would be more appropriate. The use of articles in generic statements probably constitutes a rather special use of articles, not to be subsumed in any direct fashion under the general principles discussed in the body of chapter 1 or in the above sections.

Definite expressions with relative clauses

Sometimes a speaker may use a definite expression not necessarily previously known to the listener or entailed by previous context, e.g.

(15) I just remembered what *the man I talked to at Macy's yesterday* said.

The listener may not know that the speaker talked to someone at Macy's yesterday, yet the definite expression does not cause any difficulty. The relative clause after the noun seems to introduce a specific context for the reference, so that the listener can place the referent as a unique member by its use. Often the indefinite form is relatively interchangeable with the definite form under the same circumstances:

(16) I just remembered what *a man I talked to at Macy's yesterday* said.

Sentence (15) implies more than (16) that the speaker only spoke to one man at Macy's yesterday, but no direct equivalence can be found between the use of the definite and indefinite and the uniqueness of the referent in these cases. In particular, (16) is still quite appropriate when only one man was seen. This is a complex topic (e.g. Smith, 1964) which I only mention here.

The above discussions illustrate rather well the incompleteness of the brief discussion given in chapter 1 of the use and function of articles in everyday speech. Speakers clearly have a certain range of flexibility in their referential behavior. With this much freedom in normal use, is it possible to judge, either from observation or test, whether or not someone's usage is correct? Despite obvious difficulties, I believe it is. In all semantic usage there is generally indeterminacy about the principles of usage or the scope of their application. Nevertheless, there usually exist contexts in which the boundaries of proper and improper usage are relatively clear, so that one usage is clearly preferable to another. By utilizing and devising such situations, it becomes possible to find out much about what a speaker knows by inspecting his behavior in them.

REFERENCES

Anglin, J. *The growth of word meaning.* (1970). Cambridge, Mass.: M.I.T. Press.

Bierwisch, M. (1970). Semantics. In J. Lyons (ed.), *New horizons in linguistics.* Harmondsworth, Middx.: Penguin Books.

Bloom, L., Hood, L., and Lightbown, L. (1974). Imitation in language development: if, why, and when. *Cognitive Psychology,* **6,** 380−420.

Bellugi, U. (1967). The acquisition of the system of negation in children's speech. Unpublished doctoral dissertation, Harvard University.

Brown, R. (1973). *A first language: The early stages.* Cambridge, Mass.: Harvard University Press.

Brown, R and Bellugi, U. (1964). Three processes in the child's acquisition of syntax. In E. Lenneberg (ed.), *New directions in the study of language.* Cambridge, Mass.: M.I.T. Press.

Brown, R., Cazden, C., and Bellugi, U. (1968). The child's grammar from I to III. In J. P. Hill (ed.), *Minnesota Symposium on Child Psychology,* ii, 28−73. Minneapolis, Minn.: University of Minnesota Press.

Brown, R. and Hanlon, C. (1970). Derivational complexity and order of acquisition in child speech. In J. R. Hays (ed.), *Cognition and the development of language.* New York: Wiley.

Bruner, J., Olver, R., and Greenfield, P (1966) *Studies in cognitive growth.* New York: Wiley.

Cazden, C. (1968). The acquisition of noun and verb inflections. *Child Development,* **39,** 433−48.

Clark, E. (1973). Non-linguistic strategies and the acquisition of word meanings. *Cognition,* **2,** 161−82.

Clark, E. (1974). Some aspects of the conceptual basis for first language acquisition. In R. L. Schiefelbusch and L. L. Lloyd (eds.), *Language perspectives — acquisition, retardation, and intervention*. Baltimore: University Park Press, 105—16.

Cromer, R. F. (1968). The development of temporal reference during the acquisition of language. Unpublished doctoral dissertation, Harvard University.

DeVilliers, J. G. and DeVilliers, P. A. (1974). Competence and performance in child language: are children really competent to judge? *Journal of Child Language*, **1**, 11—22.

Fernald, D. (1972). Control of grammar in imitation comprehension and production: problems of replication. *Journal of Verbal Learning and Verbal Behaviour*, **11**, 606—13.

Flavell, J. H., Botkin, P. T., Fry, C. C. Jr, Wright, J. W., and Jarvis, P. E. (1968). *The development of role-taking and communication skills in children*. New York: Wiley.

Flavell, J. H. and Wohlwill, J. F. (1969). Formal and functional aspects of cognitive development. In D. Elkind and J. H. Flavell (eds.), *Studies in cognitive development: essays in honor of Jean Piaget*, pp. 67—120. New York: Oxford University Press.

Jacobs, R. A. and Rosenbaum, P. S. (1968). *English transformational grammar*. Waltham, Mass.: Blaisdell.

Karttunen, L. (1968a). What do referential indices refer to? Santa Monica, Calif.: The Rand Corporation.

Karttunen, L. (1968b). What makes definite noun phrases definite? Santa Monica, Calif.: The Rand Corporation.

Krauss, R. M. and Glucksberg, S. (1969). The development of communication: competence as a function of age. *Child Development*, **40**, 255—66.

Lempers, J., Flavell, E., and Flavell, J. H. (1974). The development in very young children of tacit knowledge concerning visual perception. Unpublished manuscript, University of Minnesota.

Maratsos, M. P. (1971). A note on NPs made definite by entailment. *Linguistic Inquiry*, **1**, 254.

Maratsos, M. P. (1973). Nonegocentric communication abilities in preschool children. *Child Development*, **44**, 697—700.

Masangkay, Z. S., McCluskey, K. A., McIntyre, C. W., Sims-Knight, J., Vaughn, B., and Flavell, J. H. (1974). The early development of inferences about the visual percepts of others. *Child Development*, **45**, 357—66

McNeill, D. *The acquisition of language*. (1970). New York: Harper & Row, 1970.

Menyuk, P. (1963). A preliminary evaluation of grammatical capacity in children. *Journal of Verbal Learning and Verbal Behavior*, **2**, 428–39.

Mueller, E. (1973). The maintenance of verbal exchanges between young children. *Child Development*, **43**, 930–8.

Peterson, C. L. (1974). Communicative and narrative behavior of preschool-aged children. Unpublished doctoral dissertation, University of Minnesota.

Piaget, J. (1955). *The language and thought of the child*. Cleveland: Meridian Books. The World Publishing Co.

Piaget, J. *Play, dreams, and imitations*. New York: Norton, 1962.

Russell, B. (1905). On denoting. *Mind*, **14**, 479–93.

Russell, B. (1920). *Introduction to mathematical philosophy*. London: Allen and Unwin.

Shatz, M. and Gelman, R. (1973). The development of communication skills: modification in the speech of young children as a function of listener. *Monographs of the Society for Research in Child Development*, serial 152, vol. **38**, no. 5.

Smith, C. S. (1964). Determiners and relative clauses in a generative grammar of English. *Language*, **40**, 37–52.

Vendler, Z. (1967). *Linguistics and philosophy*. Ithaca, N.Y.: Cornell University Press.

INDEX

abstractness of reference: problem defined, 19—20; in young children's use of articles, 72, 94—5

Adam, Eve, and Sarah: use of articles, 15—17

adults: Cave Story results, 60; egocentrism in, 102—5

Anglin, J., 22

animacy of story referents, 76—7

articles: definite and indefinite semantics of, 1—6, 133—8; conceptual basis of, 7—13; naturalistic study of acquisition, 14—18; age of acquisition, 15—16; comprehension of, 32—5; anecdotal instances of use, 97—8. *See also* Specific—non-specific; specific reference; non-specific reference; definite reference; indefinite reference

automatic introduction of new referents: as means of comprehending indefinite expressions, 34

Bellugi, U., 15, 19

Bierwisch, M., 95

Bloom, L., 14, 25

Brown, R., 1, 2, 5, 6, 15, 16, 18, 19, 21, 25, 27, 93, 97

Bruner, J., 10, 95

Cave Story: described, 55; performance of adults vs children, 60; used to divide subjects into 3 groups, 60—1

Cazden, C., 15

classes and class membership: reference and, 3; as conceptual basis for specific—non-specific, 7—9; representations of in stories, 67—8; early competence in, 94—5

class specification: removal of, 47

competence: difficulties in estimation of, 18—19, 21—5, 96—102, 105. *See also* non-uniform competence; unity of competence

comprehension of articles: theoretical discussion, 31—5; tests described, 35—8; methodological comments on tests, 38—9; distribution of tests, 39—40, 107—10; results, 40—3; early competence in, 40—2, 72; comprehension vs production, 42—3; scores, 110—12

conversational introduction of referents: discussed, 3—4; in stories tasks, 44; stories results, 62; 4 Low group problems with, 63, 73; in games, 79—80; naturalistic anecdotes, 97—8

counterbalancing: lack of in games task, 84, 90

Cromer, R., 15

definiteness: variation in among stories, 75—7; variation in between games, 87—8

definite reference: semantics of, 1—2; entailment, 4—5; conceptual basis, 7—9; comprehension of, 32—4; paradigms used in systematic stories, 44—6

design: overall, 27—9. *See also* games; imitations with expansions; stories

discourse referents: 4, 31; means of introducing in stories, 44—5

egocentric: previous findings for young children, 10—11; in young children,